MATHS SKILLS
for
SCIENCE

YEARS 1&2
Scottish Primary 1—3

CREDITS

Author
Louise Petheram

Editor
Joel Lane

Assistant Editor
David Sandford

Series Designer
Lynne Joesbury

Designer
Rachel Warner

Cover photography
© Stockbyte

Illustrations
Debbie Clark

Published by Scholastic Ltd,
Villiers House,
Clarendon Avenue,
Leamington Spa,
Warwickshire CV32 5PR

Printed by Alden Group Ltd, Oxford

© Scholastic Ltd 2003
Text © Louise Petheram 2003

1 2 3 4 5 6 7 8 9 0   3 4 5 6 7 8 9 0 1 2

British Library Cataloguing-in-Publication Data
A catalogue record for this book is available from the British Library.

ISBN 0-439-98308-8

Teachers should consult their own school policies and guidelines concerning practical work and participation of children in scientific experiments. You should only select activities which you feel can be carried out safely and confidently in the classroom.

CONTENTS

Acknowledgements
The National Curriculum for England 2000 © Crown Copyright. Reproduced under the terms of HMSO Guidance Note 8. **The National Numeracy Strategy: Framework for Teaching Mathematics** © Crown Copyright. Reproduced under the terms of HMSO Guidance Note 8. **A Scheme of Work for Key Stages 1 and 2: Science** © Qualifications and Curriculum Authority. Reproduced under the terms of HMSO Guidance Note 8. **Scottish 5–14 Guidelines for Environmental Studies** © Crown copyright. Material is reproduced with the permission of the Controller of HMSO and the Queen's Printer for Scotland.

WHY SCIENCE NEEDS MATHS

Maths Skills for Science: Years 1 and 2/Primary 1–3) aims to assist teachers of children aged 6–7, and is one in a series of three books covering the whole primary age range. This book, and the others in the series, have been designed to develop links between the maths taught in the National Numeracy Strategy and the science topics taught in the QCA Schemes of Work, the National Curriculum for Wales, the National Curriculum for Northern Ireland and the Scottish National Guidelines on Environmental Studies 5–14. The books are thus equally valuable to teachers working in all parts of the UK.

The books recognise that for children to be effective learners, they need to develop numeracy skills and science skills in parallel. The present guidelines do not always make the links between science and maths particularly clear, and teachers often find that children need to use particular maths skills within their science lessons that they have not yet learned in their numeracy work. This forces the teacher to use science time for teaching maths skills, leading to a reduction in the 'science value' of the lessons.

Many teachers overcome this problem by co-ordinating their teaching of maths and science to ensure that the relevant maths skills are taught before they are needed in science, or that science topics are taught to reinforce skills learned in maths lessons. But the planning for this can be complicated and time-consuming. The *Maths Skills for Science* books offer a series of co-ordinated maths and science activities that do the planning for you. In addition, the skill levels of the activities are planned to ensure that:
 ▪ the science topics do not require any maths more advanced than that covered in the National Numeracy Strategy for the appropriate year
 ▪ the relevant maths skills are used and reinforced in the science topics.

"Almost every scientific investigation or experiment is likely to require one or more of the mathematical skills of classifying, counting, measuring, calculating, estimating, and recording in tables and graphs. In science pupils will, for example, order numbers, including decimals, calculate simple means and percentages, use negative numbers when taking temperatures, decide whether it is more appropriate to use a line graph or bar chart, and plot, interpret and predict from graphs."

*Introduction to the NNS **Framework for Teaching Maths**, p17 (March 1999)*

Developing the maths skills
Progression is built in throughout the series so that the children progress naturally through the skills they need to learn, consolidating and practising at each stage.

Measuring
The activities in the 'Measures' section encourage the children to think about what they need to measure, what apparatus they need to take the measurements, and whether or not the values they record will be accurate. These skills are developed throughout the three books. The children in Years 1 and 2 (Primary 2 and 3) encounter a range of different measuring apparatus and concentrate on direct comparisons, often using non-standard units that they have chosen themselves. The activities encourage them to understand the language of measurement, comparison, position and direction, and observing changes.

Handling data

Although young children may collect results successfully from their science activities, they often find it hard to decide on clear and appropriate ways to present their findings. National tests in science have shown that many children's interpretation skills lag behind their skills in other areas, and it is common for children to experience difficulty in deciding what conclusions they can draw from their work. For this reason, *Maths Skills for Science* concentrates on the whole process of making results meaningful, recognising that this process involves using both maths and science skills.

In these books, the 'Handling Data' strand of the National Numeracy Strategy has been divided into two sections: 'Recording and Organising Data' and 'Handling and Interpreting Data'. These are distinct and specific skills that all scientists need to acquire.

The 'Recording and organising data' section focuses on teaching children to think about why they are presenting their results, to identify the important features they wish to show, and to select the best way of organising their results to make these aspects clear to a reader. In the activities for Years 1&2/Primary 2–3, the children are introduced to 'concrete' methods such as grouping pictures and making picture graphs; presenting information in lists, simple tables and various pictorial forms; and explaining what these pictures are able to tell us.

In the 'Handling and interpreting data' activities, the children are challenged to ask themselves: 'What do these results really mean? What do they tell us?' Year 1 and 2 children are asked to interpret picture charts and picture graphs, answering simple questions about the data represented by the chart or graph.

ABOUT THIS BOOK

The grids on pages 8–9 show how the units in this book are linked both to the maths skills areas of the National Numeracy Strategy and to the science topics for Years 1 and 2/Primary 2–3. The science topics are taken from the QCA Schemes of Work or the corresponding documents for Scotland, Northern Ireland or Wales. The main learning objectives for both maths and science are given for each unit in the grid.

Although the units in the book cover the full range of science topics, the number dedicated to each has been varied to suit the year group. So, for example, for Year 1/Primary 2 more activities have been provided on the subjects of 'Ourselves' and 'Growing plants' than other science areas, as these are topics that very young children relate to easily. By Year 2/Primary 3, the children will be applying their increasing skills and growing awareness of the world around them to many different areas, and this is reflected in the more even spread of activities across all the science topics covered.

The activities in each book are divided into sections, based on the skill areas highlighted in the National Numeracy Strategy. In this book, the skill areas covered are:
- Numbers and the number system
- Calculation and problem solving
- Measures
- Shape and space
- Recording and organising data
- Handling and interpreting data.

At this age, the emphasis must be on reinforcing the basic number skills of understanding numbers and the number system and using this understanding to answer questions and solve problems.

The activities for each year group assume that the children will achieve approximately Level 1, Scottish Level A, at the end of Year 1/Primary 2 and Level 2, Scottish Level B, by the end of Year 2 (Primary 3). Extension activities are provided for the more able children, and there are support activities for less able children.

The activities in this book are made up of six-page units. Each unit is focuses specifically on a science topic from one of the two years covered, and uses maths skills developed within the National Numeracy Strategy for that year. Each unit is made up of two pages of teacher's notes and four supporting photocopiable pages, as detailed below.

A maths lesson planning page containing:

■ learning objectives derived from the National Numeracy Strategy

■ a suggested introduction and whole-class, teacher-directed activity

■ a follow-up children's activity consisting of individual or group work

■ ideas for differentiation for more able and less able children

■ a 'Science link' activity that provides maths resources to reinforce the skill taught in the maths lesson within a science context.

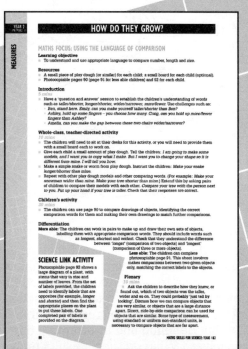

A science lesson planning page containing:

■ learning objectives derived from the QCA Schemes of Work, or the corresponding documents for Scotland, Northern Ireland or Wales

■ a suggested introduction and whole-class, teacher-directed activity

■ a follow-up children's activity consisting of individual or group work

■ ideas for differentiation for more able and less able children

■ suggested links to other subject areas within the National Curriculum.

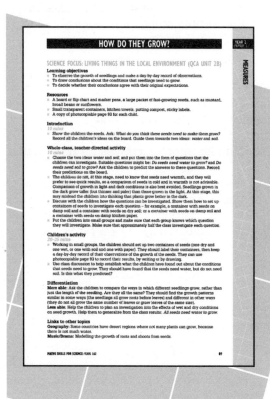

Four photocopiable worksheets:
- a pupil worksheet supporting the maths activity
- a pupil worksheet supporting the 'Science link' activity
- a pupil worksheet supporting the science activity
- a supplementary page, which may provide a supporting maths activity for less able children, or a resource or recording sheet for one of the maths or science activities.

Throughout the book, approximate times are given for the activities in both the maths and science lessons. For this age group, the lessons are intended to last a maximum of 45 minutes. However, there are opportunities to divide each lesson into two shorter sessions for very young children. In these cases, the lesson can be split into:
- first session – a slightly lengthened introduction and whole-class teacher-directed activity
- second session – a slightly shortened children's activity and plenary.

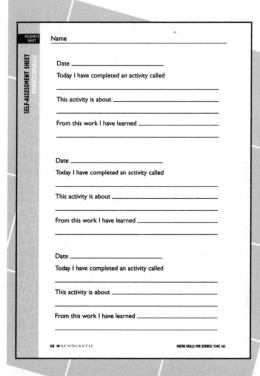

Also included at the back of the book are a number of photocopiable resource pages that can be used with several of the units. Sometimes these are listed with the resources required for individual units, but you might also find them useful in other units – or in other work altogether. These resource pages include a sheet for grouping, sheets to support the creation of pictograms, block graphs and tally charts, and a final 'pupil record sheet'.

This last page allows the children to make a note of each activity as they complete it, and to record the learning they have gained from it. The three sections on the sheet could be used by the children to record the maths activity, the 'Science link' activity and the science activity for each unit (however, other ways of organising the recording are possible).

This record also has a self-assessment function, allowing you to follow each child's developing maths skills as he or she progresses through Years 1&2/Primary 1–3), and helping you to identify children who might need particular kinds of support in forthcoming work.

YEAR 1 MATHS SKILLS AND SCIENCE TOPICS

MATHS STRANDS \ SCIENCE TOPICS	OURSELVES	GROWING PLANTS	SORTING AND USING MATERIALS	LIGHT AND DARK	PUSHES AND PULLS	SOUND AND HEARING
NUMBERS AND THE NUMBER SYSTEM	**What order do they go in?** Language of ordering. Humans change as they get older.					
CALCULATIONS AND SOLVING PROBLEMS		**Sort it out** Combining sets to make a total. Plants provide food for humans.			**Pushing and pulling** Using addition and subtraction. Pushing or pulling an object can make it move or stop.	
MEASURES						**How far away?** Measuring and comparing lengths. Comparing different sources of sound.
SHAPE AND SPACE	**Let's move** Understanding position and direction. Humans and other animals can move in many ways.	**Here and there** Using the language of position and direction. Observing different plants and where they grow.				
RECORDING AND ORGANISING DATA			**Write a list** Making lists. Water is a common material with many uses.	**Find the facts** Making lists and two-column tables. There are many sources of light.		
HANDLING AND INTERPRETING DATA	**Spot the differences** Sorting and representing in picture graphs. Differences between humans.		**Sorting materials** Representing information in pictograms. Identifying properties of materials.			

YEAR 2 MATHS SKILLS AND SCIENCE TOPICS

MATHS STRANDS \ SCIENCE TOPICS	HEALTH AND GROWTH	PLANTS AND ANIMALS IN THE LOCAL ENVIRONMENT	VARIATION	GROUPING AND CHANGING MATERIALS	FORCES AND MOVEMENT	USING ELECTRICITY
NUMBERS AND THE NUMBER SYSTEM		**Keeping a tally** Counting by making tally charts. Finding plants and animals in local habitats.				
CALCULATIONS AND SOLVING PROBLEMS			**See the pattern** Recognising patterns and relationships. Making predictions about human differences.		**Moving on** Recognising patterns and relationships. Making a fair test involving forces and their effects.	
MEASURES		**How do they grow?** Using the language of comparison. Observing the growth of seedlings.		**Changing food** Using measuring apparatus. Exploring the ways in which materials change.		
SHAPE AND SPACE				**3-D shapes** Describing 3-D shapes. Different materials have different properties.		
RECORDING AND ORGANISING DATA				**Making a table** Presenting information in a table. Exploring the properties of magnets.		
HANDLING AND INTERPRETING DATA	**Pictograms** Using a pictogram. We need exercise to stay healthy.					**Block graphs** Making a block graph. Identifying and grouping electrical appliances.

WHAT ORDER DO THEY GO IN?

MATHS FOCUS: LANGUAGE OF ORDERING

Learning objectives
■ To understand and use the language of ordering (first, last, next, before, between).
■ To understand and use the language of comparing numbers (as many as, same number as, more, fewer, most, least).
■ To respond to questions about ordering and quantity.

Resources
■ A collection of about 200 different-sized buttons (at least six different sizes), Blu-Tack.
■ Strips of stiff card (approximately 50cm × 10cm): one strip per group, plus one for the whole-class activity.
■ Coloured pencils.
■ Copies of photocopiable pages 12 (page 13 for less able children) and 14 for each child.

Introduction
Up to 5 mins
■ Show the children a selection of 20–30 buttons. Count them together. *How are they the same? How are they different?*

Whole-class, teacher-directed activity
10 mins
■ Ask a child to put about six different buttons in order. Let the child decide how (if the buttons are of various sizes, he or she will almost certainly put them in order of size). Display the buttons Blu-Tacked to a strip of card. *How could we describe the order of the buttons? Which button comes first? Which comes last? What colour is the middle one?* Make sure the children understand the difference between ordering and grouping. If the child chose an order not based on size, reorder the buttons according to size and discuss this order.
■ Show the children a button of an intermediate size. *Where shall we put this one?* Help them to decide the correct position. Blu-Tack it onto the card.
■ Show the children a button the same size as one already on the card. *Where shall we put this one?* Help them to decide that it must share a place with a button already in the order. Repeat this with several buttons of different sizes.

Children's activity
20–25 mins
■ Divide the class into small groups. Give each group a selection of 20 or more buttons in five distinct sizes. Ask them to put the buttons in order, then to record which buttons were in first, third and fifth place on their own copy of photocopiable page 12, answering the questions on the sheet.

SCIENCE LINK ACTIVITY
Photocopiable page 14 shows six different-coloured pencils for the children to colour in and then put in order of length. The length of each pencil is shown by the number of blocks beside it. The children then answer questions about the order the pencils are in.

Differentiation
More able: Ask the children to order their buttons in a different way (such as by the number of holes), and to write a short sentence to describe this order. Ask: *Is the number of buttons in the first/ last place the same as it was before?*
Less able: The children could use 10–20 buttons in only three distinct sizes. Photocopiable page 13 has questions relating to this task.

Plenary
10 mins
■ Show the children a set of buttons in order. Check their understanding of words such as *first, last, between, middle, most, least.* Discuss other things that can be ordered, such as: story books in order of size on a shelf; shoes in order of size in the cloakroom; children in order of age in the register.

SCIENCE FOCUS: OURSELVES (QCA UNIT 1A)

Learning objectives
- To know that all animals, including humans, grow and change as they become older.
- To ask questions and make suggestions about the ways humans change as they get older.
- To make observations and comparisons of height.

Resources
- Squares of card (10cm × 10cm) with the name of each child and his or her position in the class based on age order (1 for youngest, 30 for oldest) written on.
- Photographs of people of different ages.
- Height charts, bathroom scales.
- A copy of photocopiable page 15 for each child.

Introduction
Up to 5 mins
- Discuss the ways that people and other animals change as they get older. Ask children with younger or older siblings how they are different in terms of size and what they can do. Ask children with a puppy or a kitten at home to compare these with an adult dog or cat.

Whole-class, teacher-directed activity
10 mins
- Display photographs of people at different ages. Help the children to rearrange the photographs in order of age, the youngest first. *How can you tell?*
- Find out the children's birthdays and sort them into age order. (Make sure you already have a record of the children in age order, with their birthday dates: many children may not know the date of their birthday.)
- Give each child a card with his or her name and number in the order of class ages (see 'Resources'). (Putting names on the cards will help to prevent confusion if cards are dropped. Numbering the youngest as 1 might lead the children to look for a pattern of height increasing as the number increases. This pattern is unlikely to exist, as the older children in the class are not necessarily taller.)
- Ask the children to predict how their height (and/or their weight) will change as they get older.

Children's activity
20–25 mins
- The children can work in groups of five or six, ordering themselves according to age with the youngest first (numbers on cards ascending). They can record the order on photocopiable page 15, using stick drawings with names. Then they can order themselves according to height, with the shortest first (either by direct comparison or by using a height chart to measure each child), and record this order in the same way. Ask each group: *Are the two orders the same? Was your prediction about height and age right?* Alternatively, some groups could order themselves by weight – either by direct comparison (using a see-saw) or by measuring with bathroom scales.

Differentiation
More able: Ask the children to compare their heights by measuring with a height chart, and to find the difference in height between the shortest and the tallest in the group. Can they find a child about halfway between the shortest and tallest children?
Less able: Give the children new cards showing the age order (with the youngest as 1) within their group. Help them to find the height order using direct comparison.

Links to other topics
Music: Listen to music getting louder or quieter.
Art: Paint or draw pictures with colours getting darker to show shadows.
History: How clothes, cars, houses and toys have changed with time.

WHAT ORDER DO THEY GO IN?

Put them in order

■ Count all your buttons.
How many are there?

■ Put your buttons in order of size.

■ Which buttons were in first place? Draw round them.

■ Which buttons were in last place? Draw round them.

■ Draw round the buttons that were in third place.

Which place had the most buttons? _____

How many were there? _____

NOW TRY THIS Can you put your buttons in a different order? Tell your teacher what the order is.

MATHS SKILLS FOR SCIENCE: YEARS 1&2

Put them in order

▪ Count all your buttons.
How many are there?

▪ Put your buttons in order
of size in the box below.

▪ Draw round them.

First place	Middle place	Last place

How many buttons are in first place? _____

Which place has the most buttons:
first place, middle place or last place? _____

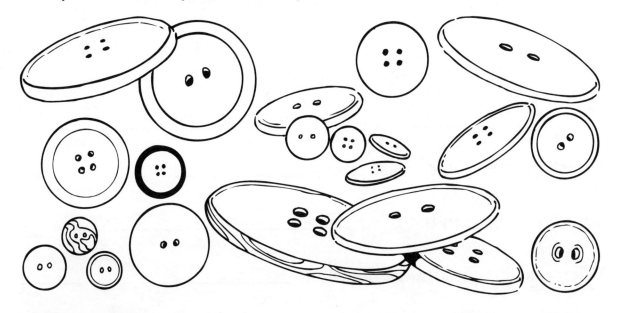

WHAT ORDER DO THEY GO IN?

Shortest to longest

■ Colour these pencils. Use the right colour for each pencil.

■ Draw them in order of length, with the shortest first.

Which colour is in the last place? _____

Which colour is in the third place? _____

What place is the orange pencil in? _____

How tall are we?

■ Use stick drawings to draw the children in your group in order of age.

■ Use stick drawings to draw the children in your group in order of height.

Are these two orders the same for your group? _____

What is the difference in height between the tallest child and the

shortest child? _____

Whose height is in the middle? _____

SORT IT OUT

MATHS FOCUS: COMBINING SETS TO MAKE A TOTAL

Learning objectives
- To understand addition as combining sets.
- To use addition vocabulary (sum, total, altogether) in practical contexts.
- To understand that more than two numbers can be added together.
- To use the knowledge that addition can be done in any order.

Resources
- Plastic storage trays with compartments, a selection of up to 20 objects that can be grouped in several ways (buttons or building blocks in different colours and shapes; LEGO bricks in different colours and sizes), a selection of red and blue beads.
- Coloured pencils and/or pens, labels, a number line.
- Photocopiable pages 18 (page 19 for less able children) and 20 for each child.

Introduction
5 mins
- Ask some oral addition questions, including simple problems for the more able children: *4 add 2, add 3 to 2, 5 plus 1. What is the total of 5 and 3? I have 4 sweets in one pocket and 3 sweets in the other. How many sweets do I have? I think of a number, then add 4. I have 8. What number did I think of?*

Whole-class, teacher-directed activity
10 mins
- Discuss the different ways in which your selection of objects could be 'tidied away' into a storage tray, such as: big beads, medium beads and small beads; red bricks, blue bricks, green bricks and yellow bricks.
- Ask: *How many beads are there in the tray altogether? How can we find out without tipping them all out again?*
- Count the objects in each compartment. Use a label to show the number in each compartment. Add these numbers, using a number line or fingers. Check the sum by tipping all the objects out and counting them.
- Repeat with a different way of sorting the objects.

Children's activity
20–25 mins
- Ask the children to find, and record on a copy of photocopiable page 18, two different ways of arranging your selection of objects (for example, by colour or by shape). Ask them to use the combination of sets to find the total each time.

Differentiation
More able: Ask the children to investigate problems that involve partitioning a set of 7 objects into 3 sets. Ask: *How many ways can you add together 3 numbers to make a total of 7?* They can represent their answers by drawing the objects or by writing the sums.

Less able: Ask the children to sort only red and blue beads (with a total of 10 or less), using photocopiable page 19. They can practise sorting other groups of beads, using two different colours or shapes.

SCIENCE LINK ACTIVITY

Photocopiable page 20 shows the variety of plant foods eaten by a child. Ask the children to identify the plant foods they eat, and then to sort them according to when they would eat them. Encourage them to use the 'combination of sets' method to find the total number of plant foods eaten.

Plenary
10 mins
- Look at some of the ways the children grouped their objects. Ask other children to check some of the totals, using either mental arithmetic or apparatus. Were the totals correct? Display some of the work until the next lesson.

SCIENCE FOCUS: GROWING PLANTS (QCA UNIT 1B)

Learning objectives
- To be aware that many different plants provide food for humans.
- To know that plants have leaves, roots, stems, flowers and fruits.

Resources
- Samples (or packages) of foods from plants. (Include some that are not obviously plants, such as cereals or bread.)
- Pictures of foods from plants from old gardening, cookery or supermarket magazines, a flip chart or board, markers, Blu-Tack.
- Child-safe scissors, adhesive, pencils, coloured pens.
- Copies of photocopiable page 21 and resource page 124 for each child or group.

Introduction
5 mins
- Ask: *Do you eat plants? What plants do you eat?* Help the children to name as many foods from plants as they can.

Whole-class, teacher-directed activity
10 mins
- Draw a large plant (such as an apple tree) on the flip chart. Show clearly its leaves, roots, stem and fruits. Together, stick cut-out pictures of plant foods on the flip chart with Blu-Tack (so that the pictures can be rearranged) to show which part of the plant they have come from. Include some processed plant foods such as orange juice and tinned peas.
- Ask: *How can we sort these foods into groups?* Look at different ways of grouping them, such as:
  - those eaten at particular mealtimes
  - those eaten every day or only sometimes
  - those that come from different parts of the plant.
- Discuss how the children could find out how many different plant foods they eat: by grouping them, counting how many there are in each group, then using mental arithmetic or apparatus to add all the groups together.

Children's activity
20–25 mins
- Photocopiable page 21 gives instructions for this activity. The children can cut out magazine pictures of 'plant' foods that they eat, then decide how these foods can be grouped. They could use one of the groupings discussed in the lesson introduction, or a different idea of their own. They should record their groups on a copy of resource page 124, either by drawing or by cutting out the pictures and sticking them on. Ask them to find the total number of plant foods they eat by combining the sets.

Differentiation
More able: The children can find alternative ways of grouping the foods they eat – for example, foods they like a lot, like a little bit or don't like at all. They could plan a shopping list for their family for one day, or to provide lunch for all the children on their table.
Less able: Encourage the children to sort the 'plant' foods into just two groups – for example, those they like and those they don't, or those that come in packets and those that don't.

Links to other topics
Ourselves: Do the children all like the same fruit and vegetables? Include a tasting session for different fruits (including exotic ones) or a 'healthy snack day' in a topic on healthy eating.
People who help us: The children can use videos, books or the Internet to find out about the work of farmers, market gardeners, shopkeepers, school cooks and others who grow and prepare food.

SORT IT OUT

How many altogether?

■ Draw your groups.

How many? ☐	How many? ☐
How many? ☐	How many? ☐

How many altogether?

■ Group them in a different way.

How many? ☐	How many? ☐
How many? ☐	How many? ☐

How many altogether?

NOW TRY THIS How many different ways can you find to sort 7 buttons into 3 groups?

How many beads?

■ Count all your beads.

How many are there? _____

■ Draw the beads in these groups:

Red beads	Blue beads
How many? [ ]	How many? [ ]

How many beads are there altogether? _____

■ Write a sum to show how you worked it out.

NOW TRY THIS Sort some more beads into groups.
Draw your groups on the back of this sheet.

CALCULATIONS AND SOLVING PROBLEMS

PHOTOCOPIABLE

Eating plants

Here are all the different plants that Sayeed eats.

orange juice

tomatoes

apple

jam

lettuce

banana

blackcurrant drink

potatoes

carrots

fruit yoghurt

grapes

bread

cereal

peanuts

crisps

vegetable soup

■ Circle the plant foods that you eat too.
When do you eat them? Write them in this table.

Breakfast time	Lunch time
Tea time	Snacks

NOW TRY THIS How many plant foods do you eat altogether?
■ Write a sum to show how you worked it out.

What plants do you eat?

- Cut out some pictures of different plants that you eat.
- Sort your plant food pictures into groups.
- Write the names of your groups on your recording sheet.

- Stick your plant pictures into the right boxes.
  How many plant foods do you eat altogether?
- Write a sum to show how you worked it out.

NOW TRY THIS

Could you group the plants that you eat in a different way?

CALCULATIONS AND SOLVING PROBLEMS

PUSHING AND PULLING

MATHS FOCUS: USING ADDITION AND SUBTRACTION

Learning objectives
- To use the operations of addition and subtraction.
- To use a number line to explore addition and subtraction problems.

Resources
- Marker pens, large counters, Blu-Tack, flashcards numbered 1–20.
- Individual 0–20 number lines, a metre ruler marked into 20 equal sections. (Cut 10 strips of coloured paper 5cm wide. Use adhesive tape to stick them to the metre ruler as shown in the diagram below.)
- Photocopiable pages 24 (page 25 for less able children) and 26 for each child.

leave blank   coloured paper stuck on

Introduction
5 mins
- Count and clap from 0 to 20 together. Repeat, missing out some numbers with the children filling these in. Try counting and clapping backwards from 10 to 0 together.

Whole-class, teacher-directed activity
10 mins
- Show the children the 0–20 number line (marked metre rule). Count along it, writing in some of the numbers. Ask children to work out what numbers should go in the blank spaces.
- Fasten a large counter to the metre rule with Blu-Tack. Ask: *Where will I end up if I add on 3? Take off 4? Add on 5? Subtract 2?* Ask the children to work out the answers by imagining the counter moving. Use differentiated questions to allow all the children to answer.
- Fasten the counter as before. Ask: *What must I do to land on 12? 6? 19?* The children should work out the answers as before. Again, use differentiated questions.

Children's activity
20–25 mins
- Working individually, the children can complete photocopiable page 24. Allow them to use individual number lines and counters to solve the problems, but do not discourage them from using mental methods or fingers if these are providing the correct answers. The children can then use number lines or counters to explore all the different ways of using two numbers to make a total of a number you set them.

Differentiation
More able: Give the children a harder number to make as a total. If appropriate, encourage them to use subtraction as well (for example, making 12 as '17 take away 5').

Less able: The children can use photocopiable page 25. When they have completed the sheet, set them a problem that reinforces number bonds to 5 or to 10 (for example, 'Find all the pairs of numbers that add together to make 5'.)

SCIENCE LINK ACTIVITY

The children can use photocopiable page 26 to practise using addition and subtraction to solve problems. They have to imagine pushing a monkey up a tree (a vertical number line) or pulling him down in order to make him stop at certain numbers. Talk through the answer to the first problem: *How would you make Bojo move from 15 to 18?* 'Push him up 3'.

Plenary
10 mins
- Display the 0–20 number line. Hold up pairs of flashcards with a small number and a larger number. Each time, the children have to work out how to get from the smaller number to the larger (for example, 'add 3'). If appropriate, repeat with subtraction: the children have to work out how to get from a large number to a smaller number (for example, 'take away 3').

MATHS SKILLS FOR SCIENCE: YEARS 1&2

PUSHING AND PULLING

SCIENCE FOCUS: PUSHES AND PULLS (QCA UNIT 1E)

Learning objectives

■ To be aware that pushing or pulling objects can make them start or stop moving.
■ To make suggestions about how objects can be made to move, and to find out whether they were right.

Resources

■ An example or picture of a door with 'Push' and 'Pull' signs.
■ A selection of objects of varying mass, shoe boxes.
■ A selection of toys operated by pushes or pulls (you could include some toys operated by twists for more able children), sticky labels, A4 paper.
■ A copy of photocopiable page 27 for each child

Introduction

5 mins

■ Ask volunteers: *Push on my hand. Pull on my hand.* Make sure all the children know the difference between a push and a pull. Show them the door (or picture of a door) with 'Push' and 'Pull' signs. *How would you open this door?* Go to the other side of the door (or show the other sign). *How would you open it now?*

Whole-class, teacher-directed activity

5 mins

■ Display a small selection of shoe boxes, each containing a different-sized object (use some heavy objects and some light objects). Ask volunteers to push the boxes gently. *What happens to them when they are pushed?* Establish that the objects move when they are pushed. *Which object do you think is the hardest to move?* Ask the child who answers to test his or her prediction. Help the children to understand that the heaviest object needs the biggest push to make it move.
■ Repeat the activity above, but this time using pulls instead of pushes.
■ Discuss the safety of pushing and pulling various objects. Tell the children that they must not try to push or pull things that are hard to move. If the object does move, it may hurt someone.

Children's activity

20–25 mins

■ Working in small groups, the children should search the classroom for objects that can be moved by a push (such as an open door) or a pull (such as a shut drawer). Remind them to include objects that might only move a little bit (such as adhesive tape stuck to a desk).
■ The children should record the objects they find, either by attaching a sticky label to each object saying 'Push' or 'Pull', or by drawing on a copy of photocopiable page 27. At the end of page 27, the children are asked to choose a toy and to predict how they could make it move. They can record their prediction, then test the toy to see whether they were right.

Differentiation

More able: Give the children slightly more complicated toys. If appropriate, you could include a toy that needs a twist – a push and a pull at the same time. (Ask children to imagine how two mice would make the toy work: one would push and the other would pull.)
Less able: Ask the children to find just two objects needing a push and two objects needing a pull. Give them a toy requiring a simple push or pull to make it move.

Links to other topics

Ourselves: Safety in the playground or park – the danger to children of moving swings and see-saws, people on skateboards, and so on.
PE and drama: Modelling the movement of objects that have been pushed or pulled.

PUSHING AND PULLING

Add and take away problems

■ Use a number line. Start at 6 and add on 3.

6 add on 3
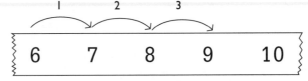

■ Write the sum.   6 + 3 = _____

■ Now use a number line to solve these problems. Write the sum or the 'take away' each time.

4 add on 5   _____

8 add on 7   _____

18 take away 2   _____

14 take away 5   _____

■ Look at this problem.

Start at 14. Add on 2.

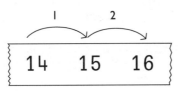

■ Now try these.

Start at 10. Go to 17. How many steps? _____

Start at 10. Go to 6. How many steps? _____

NOW TRY THIS   Think of different ways to land on 16. Write them out, using 'Start on…' and 'Add on…' or 'Take away…'

Add on and take away

▨ Use a number line. Start at 3 and add on 2.

3 add on 2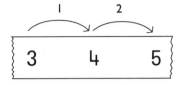

▨ Write the sum.   3 + 2 = _____

▨ Now do these. Use a number line, then write the sums.

4 add on 1   _____

6 add on 4   _____

7 add on 3   _____

▨ Now do some 'take aways'. Use a number line.

10 take away 2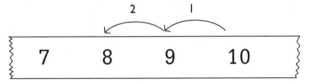

▨ Write the 'take away'.   10 – 2 = _____

▨ Now do these. Write the 'take aways'.

10 take away 3   _____

10 take away 4   _____

10 take away 5   _____

PUSHING AND PULLING

Up and down the number tree

▨ Bojo the monkey is too lazy to move. You have to push him up the tree or pull him down.

Push him up.

Pull him down.

▨ Write how you would make Bojo move:

from 15 to 18 _____

from 12 to 9 _____

from 7 to 13 _____

from 19 to 11 _____

from 4 to 15 _____

20
19
18
17
16
15
14
13
12
11
10
9
8
7
6
5
4
3
2
1
0

Making things move

▨ Draw two things that move when you push them.

▨ Draw two things that move when you pull them.

▨ List more things that move when you push or pull them.

Push	Pull

 NOW TRY THIS Choose **one** toy. Draw a picture to show how you could make it move. Try out your idea. Were you right?

HOW FAR AWAY?

MEASURES

MATHS FOCUS: MEASURING AND COMPARING LENGTHS

Learning objectives
- To understand and use vocabulary related to length.
- To measure lengths and compare them directly.
- To use simple measuring equipment, such as string or ribbon, to compare lengths.

Resources
- Objects to be grouped according to height or length (such as ribbons, vases, books, teddies), string, adhesive.
- Pencils, A4 or lining paper, child-safe scissors.
- Photocopiable pages 30 (page 31 for less able) and 32 for each child or pair.

Introduction
5 mins
- Ask questions using the language of comparison, such as: *Which book is taller/shorter? Which row of bricks is longer/shorter? Which child* [of two] *is closer to/further from the door?*

Whole-class, teacher-directed activity
10 mins
- Talk about the relative sizes of three or more similar objects. Talk about their heights or lengths, encouraging the children to use precise words such as *tall(er)*, *short(er)* and *long(er)* rather than the more vague *big(ger)* and *small(er)*. Show how 'tall' becomes 'long' when an object is laid on its side.
- Discuss how to find the tallest or longest of several objects: *How can we find the next tallest/longest?* Help the children to arrange the objects in order by using direct comparison.
- Ask: *How can we find out which cupboard is taller?* (Choose two objects that clearly cannot be put side by side for direct comparison.) Show the children how to use string as a relative measure of height, width or length: cut two lengths of string, then compare them.

Children's activities
15–20 mins
1. The children can work in small groups, using direct comparison to arrange their group in order of height. Ask them to record by drawing the children in their group in order from the tallest to the shortest. Alternatively, let them draw around each other on lining paper, then make and order life-sized cut-outs for a display.
2. The children can use string to compare the lengths of the caterpillars shown on photocopiable page 30. They can then cut out the caterpillar pictures and stick them in order of length (shortest to longest) on another sheet of paper, together with the string they used for measuring each caterpillar.

SCIENCE LINK ACTIVITY

Photocopiable page 32 shows the distances at which three characters can *just* hear different sounds. The children can compare these distances by counting the number of 'steps' shown in order to decide which sound source is the loudest. As an extension, ask the children which chair a fourth character should sit on in order to hear a particular sound.

Differentiation
More able: Ask the children to find other things that can be compared using string. Encourage them to find things they could not measure directly with a ruler. Ask them to record what they measured and to glue the string to the paper to show how long it was.

Less able: Give the children copies of page 31 to complete, supporting them as necessary to compare the lengths using string.

Plenary
10 mins
- Look at some of the children's work. Are the children shown in the correct height order? Use the drawings to give practice in finding someone 'taller than Ben' or 'shorter than Kate'. Ask them to show the class some of the other objects they have compared using string.

SCIENCE FOCUS: SOUND AND HEARING (QCA UNIT 1F)

Learning objectives
- To know that there are many different sources of sounds.
- To realise that sounds are louder when you are nearer the source, and become fainter as you travel away from the source.
- To measure distances using non-standard (or standard) measures.

Resources
- Three or four different sources of sound, such as a clock with a loud tick, a metronome or a tape recording of music. (Choose sound sources where the volume will stay fairly constant, not objects such as drums where the sound volume depends on how hard the object is hit.)
- Various measures, such as 30cm rulers, metre rulers, tape measures and string.
- Pictures of various different sound sources, a large sheet of paper, glue or Blu-Tack.
- A copy of photocopiable page 33 for each child.

Introduction
5 mins
- *What things make sounds?* Help the children to think of a wide range of sound sources, such as musical instruments, people, radios, cars and doorbells.

Whole-class, teacher-directed activity
10 mins
- Write the word 'sound' in the middle of a large sheet of paper. Ask: *How do we describe sounds?* Write the words *loud, quiet, high, low, ringing* and so on on the sheet, adding pictures of appropriate sound sources if possible.
- Discuss how sounds further away are quieter. *Can you hear Mrs Smith's class? Do you think Mrs Smith can? Tom, can you hear Cassie's watch ticking? Put it to his ear, Cassie. Can you hear it now, Tom?*
- *How can we find out how far away a sound can be before we can't hear it any more?* If necessary, suggest walking away until they can only just hear the sound, then measuring the distance by counting the steps, using string or counting the number of (metre) rulers used.
- Practise measuring this distance with one or two sound sources. Emphasise the importance of moving each time until you can only just hear the sound. You might like to introduce the idea that this makes it a fair test for all the sounds.

Children's activity
25–30 mins
- Give the children a range of different sound sources, some loud and some quiet. Ask them to choose a suitable way to measure distances from the sound source. They could use steps, string, ruler lengths or other uniform non-standard measures.
- The children can then use photocopiable page 33 to record the distance from which different sound sources can be heard, then use these measurements to decide which sound is the loudest or quietest.

Differentiation
More able: Encourage the children to decide on the most appropriate measuring equipment to measure the distances to the different sound sources. They can use this to measure the distances using standard units.
Less able: Tell the children what uniform non-standard units they should use to measure the distances, such as steps or ruler lengths. Alternatively, it may be appropriate to help them suggest and choose suitable non-standard units of their own.

Links to other topics
Citizenship: Noise pollution – what sounds are unpleasant or a nuisance (mobile phones, pneumatic road drills)?
Music/PE: The children can find or make sounds appropriate to different actions or moods, or vice versa.

MEASURES

PHOTOCOPIABLE

Caterpillars

How long are these caterpillars?

■ Use string to compare them.

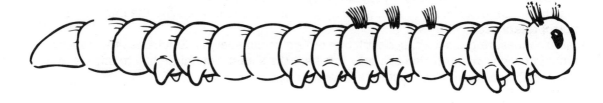

■ Cut out the caterpillars.

■ Stick them in order of length on another sheet of paper.

NOW TRY THIS Can you use string to compare other things?

Long and short caterpillars

▨ How long is this caterpillar? Use string to measure it.

Which of these caterpillars are longer than the one above?

▨ Colour them in.

Which caterpillar is the longest?
▨ Give him a big smile.

Which string did you use to measure the longest caterpillar?
▨ Stick the string here.

Loud and quiet sounds

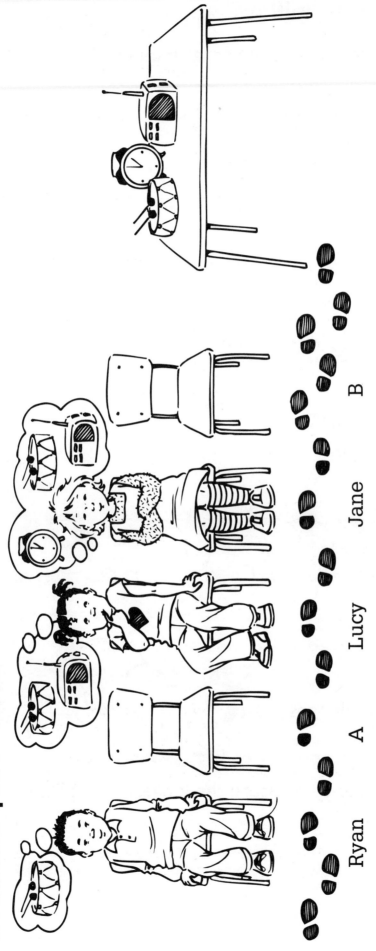

Ryan   A   Lucy   Jane   B

The pictures above each child show which sounds that child can hear.

Who can hear the most sounds? _____

Which sound is the quietest? _____   Which sound is the loudest? _____

Tom wants to hear the radio but **not** the clock. Which chair should he sit on, A or B? _____

The loudest sound

Gemma can **just** hear the clock.

▨ Draw your sounds in this table.

Sound	Distance

▨ Measure the distance between you and each sound when you can only just hear it.

Which sound is the loudest? _____

Which sound is the quietest? _____

NOW TRY THIS Which of these is the best way to measure distances? Use it to measure the distance to your loudest sound.

LET'S MOVE

MATHS FOCUS: UNDERSTANDING POSITION AND DIRECTION

Learning objectives
- To use everyday language to describe position.
- To use everyday language to describe direction.
- To recognise and use everyday language to describe movement.

Resources
- For each group: a selection of large and small objects (pencil pots, pencil sharpeners, erasers and so on), a small LEGO figure or doll's house doll, coloured pencils.
- Photocopiable page 36 (enlarged on card if possible), cut into individual cards.
- Photocopiable pages 37 and 38 for each child.

Introduction
5 mins
- This lesson is about using appropriate vocabulary to describe position and direction. Begin with a session of questions, instructions and responses: *Who is sitting next to Sakina? Hannah, go and sit between Mark and Gul. What is above the door? John, face towards the computer. Anya, move away from the radiator.*

Whole-class, teacher-directed activity
15 mins
- Help the children to follow a 'Mystery trail' around the classroom. You can either use the cards on photocopiable page 36 or invent your own. All of the cards should be quite easy to find in the classroom. Select a child to carry out the instruction on the first card, and to bring the second card back to you. A second child should carry out the second instruction and bring back the third card, and so on.
  - 1st card *(hold in your hand)*: reads 'Next to the door'.
  - 2nd card *(place next to the door)*: reads 'Under the window'.
  - 3rd card *(place under the window)*: reads 'Above the computer'.
  - 4th card *(place above the computer)*: reads 'Behind the pencils'.
  - 5th card *(place behind the pencils)*: reads 'Beside the board'.
  - 6th card *(place beside the board)*: reads 'On the teacher's chair'.
- Place a small 'treasure' on your chair, such as a book or some stickers for the children.

Children's activity
20 mins
- Give each group some large and small objects (see 'Resources'). The children take turns to place a small LEGO figure or doll's house doll among the objects. Another child describes the figure's position, using words such as 'behind', 'under' and 'next to'. The others decide whether the description is correct.
- The children can complete page 37 individually.

SCIENCE LINK ACTIVITY

This activity links the vocabulary of movement to the science of how animals move. The children can use photocopiable page 38 to draw animals and people moving, and choose appropriate words to describe the animal movements. This can be followed by a PE lesson in which the children follow your instructions by moving in particular ways (walking, crawling, hopping and so on) and in particular directions.

Differentiation
More able: The children can extend the description of the doll's position to include two or more statements, such as: *It is next to the pencil sharpener and behind the pencil pot.* Can they describe the patterns on the mittens?
Less able: If possible, provide adult help with the describing activity, or put the children in mixed-ability groups and ask them to help each other. Use a smaller number of objects per group.

Plenary
10 mins
- Recap on the meanings of various position and direction words. Ask children (one at a time) to direct a volunteer to a particular place or object.

SCIENCE FOCUS: OURSELVES (QCA UNIT 1A)

Learning objectives
- To know that animals, including humans, move.
- To make observations and comparisons of the ways that animals move.

Resources
- A video showing different types of animal (preferably including humans) moving.
- Space for PE activities, a tape player and tape of different styles of music (suitable for different types of movement).
- Large sheets of paper, coloured pencils or paints, collage materials.
- A copy of photocopiable page 39 for each child.

Introduction
10–15 mins
- Talk to the children about the ways they move. Ask them to think of some words to describe different ways that they move. Good words might include *running, walking, crawling, hopping, jumping, rolling, sliding*. Encourage the children to think of as many as possible.
- Talk about words to do with position and direction, such as *forwards, backwards, sideways, round, up, down*. Again, encourage the children to think of as many words as possible.
- Watch a video of animals moving. Talk about and describe each animal's movement. *How is it like the way we move? How is it different?* Introduce words such as *fast, slow, slithering, gliding, flapping*.

Whole-class, teacher-directed activity
20–25 mins
- This activity can be done in a PE lesson. Ask the children to think of different ways in which they can move: walking, running and so on. Ask all the children to practise moving in the ways described. Encourage them to think of, describe and demonstrate ways in which they can move different parts of their bodies, and ways in which they can change direction.
- Ask the children to work in small groups, planning a sequence of three moves to show some of the different ways that humans can move. They should include a movement that is slow, a movement that is fast and at least one change of direction. The groups can take turns to demonstrate their sequence of moves to the rest of the class, and use words such as *jumping, hopping* and *turning* to describe what they are doing. They could make large-scale drawings, paintings or collages to form part of a display on position and movement.

Children's activity
15 mins
- After the PE activity, the children can use photocopiable page 39 to label pictures showing different types of movement. They can then draw themselves moving in one of the ways they have used in the PE activity, and choose suitable words to label their drawing.

Differentiation
More able: Encourage the children to make full use of their language skills, introducing words such as *twist, slide, curve, around* and possibly even *left* and *right*.
Less able: Encourage the children to design a short sequence of moves that can be described with the basic vocabulary of position and movement: *fast, slow, up, down, towards, away from*.

Links to other topics
Literacy: Speaking and listening – this activity gives children an opportunity to practise listening to, following and planning a series of instructions.
Citizenship: There are opportunities here to discuss ways of working safely together, with consideration for others, when many children are all moving about (sometimes quickly) in a relatively small space.
Music: The children can listen to and choose types of music that are suitable for different types of movement.

Mystery trail labels

Next to the door.

Under the window.

Above the computer.

Behind the pencils.

Beside the board.

On the teacher's chair.

Where are the mittens?

swings

climbing frame

see-saw

sandpit

slide

Four mittens have been dropped in the playground.

Draw these mittens in the picture:

Under the see-saw. Colour the mitten blue.

Beside the swings. Colour the mitten red.

On the slide. Colour the mitten yellow.

Next to the sandpit. Colour the mitten green.

Draw an orange mitten somewhere in the playground.

Where is it? _____

NOW TRY THIS Can you describe the patterns on the mittens to your teacher?

LET'S MOVE

Animal movements

■ Draw three animals that move in different ways.

How do they move?
■ Write some describing words next to them.

Jack is running fast.

■ Draw something he is running away from.
■ Draw something he is running towards.

How we move

These children are all moving.

▦ Label the children, using these movement words.

run	slide	jump	hop	crawl	roll

▦ Draw a picture of yourself moving in a PE lesson.
▦ Label your picture with words that say how you are moving.

HERE AND THERE

MATHS FOCUS: UNDERSTANDING POSITION AND DIRECTION

Learning objectives

■ To use everyday language to describe the position of an object.
■ To use everyday language to describe direction.

Resources

■ A glove puppet.
■ Beanbags in four different colours, small balls in four different colours.
■ A board or flip chart and marker pens.
■ Photocopiable pages 42 (page 43 for less able children) and 44 for each child.

Introduction

5 mins

■ Ask: *What words can we use to describe where something is?* Give the children some examples, such as: *next to, beside, under, near.* Help each child to make a short sentence to describe where he or she is: 'I am near the chair', 'I am next to Robert' and so on.

Whole-class, teacher-directed activity

5–10 mins

■ Help the children to make a list of position and direction words and phrases on the board (*far away from, near, beside, under, going towards, going away from* and so on).
■ Show the children the glove puppet. Put it in a particular place, or move it in a particular direction. Ask for volunteers to describe where it is or how it is moving, using one of the words or phrases in your list. Ask for several volunteers to make sentences about the glove puppet, using as many appropriate position and direction words as possible. Repeat with a different position or direction.

Children's activity

20–25 mins

■ Position the beanbags and small balls in clearly visible positions around the classroom. The children can use copies of photocopiable page 42 to describe the positions of the beanbags.

Differentiation

More able: Ask the children to draw the position of one of the coloured balls (as an extension to page 42). They can write appropriate labels around it to describe its position, such as *under the shelf, on the computer, next to the book or beside the pencils.* Ask them to write as many different labels as they can think of.

Less able: The children can complete photocopiable page 43. Explain the meanings of the position and direction words to them if necessary.

SCIENCE LINK ACTIVITY

Photocopiable page 44 shows a map of a 'Pirate island'. The children have to understand the vocabulary of position and direction in order to find particular objects and locations, and follow instructions to reach the 'treasure'.

Plenary

10 mins

■ Ask the children to show their work and make up sentences to describe some of their drawings, such as: 'I have drawn the computer under the yellow beanbag.' 'I drew the window to show that it is far away from the blue beanbag.' Other children can judge whether they were correct, and suggest other things that could have been drawn as well. Ask questions such as: *Can you think of anything else that is far away from the blue beanbag?*

MATHS SKILLS FOR SCIENCE: YEARS 1&2

SCIENCE FOCUS: GROWING PLANTS (QCA UNIT 1B)

Learning objectives
- To know that there are different plants in the immediate environment.
- To treat growing plants with care.
- To make careful observations of plants and where they are growing.

Resources
- A picture or sample of a plant, showing leaves, stem and flowers.
- Access to the school grounds or a local area with a range of different habitats (path, grass, flower bed, field and so on).
- A large plan (with room for all the children to stick pictures on) of the local area you will visit.
- Clipboards, pencils, coloured pencils, scissors, adhesive. Sufficient adult help to supervise the children drawing plants in different parts of the area you will visit.
- A poster showing different plants in a habitat (such as woodland, a meadow or a pond).
- A copy of photocopiable page 45 for each child.

Introduction
10 mins
- Ask: *Where have you seen plants? What are they like?* Discuss where the children have seen plants growing. Show them the picture or sample of a plant and help them to identify its main parts. Show them the poster of plants in a habitat and ask: *Are all these plants the same?* Help them to identify some general types of plants, such as trees, grass, bushes or pond plants. Ask them to look at a few specific plants in more detail. Help them to identify or name some plants they are familiar with, such as dandelions and daisies.

Whole-class, teacher-directed activity
15 mins
- Take the children around the school grounds or local area. Ask them to find plants in as many places as they can. They can use photocopiable page 45 to record (using words or pictures) where they saw plants growing, but they should not pick or pull up the plants.
- Ask the children to make a drawing of one of the plants they find. It can be a familiar one or one they don't recognise. They should include as much detail as they can, and colour their picture. They can use the bottom section of photocopiable page 45 to make a drawing of one specific plant.

Children's activity
15 mins
- A picture or sample of a plant, showing leaves, stem and flowers. Back in the classroom, the children can cut out their drawing of a plant. They can work in groups, with each child telling the others what his or her plant is (if known) and where it was found. The children in the group can then decide together where each picture should go on the large plan of the school grounds or local area, and stick it in place.

Differentiation
More able: The children can work in groups to discuss where various types of plants grow in the school grounds or local area, and what each type is like. For example, did they find any plants with flowers, or with seeds? Where do most of a given type of plant seem to grow: in the middle of the field or next to the path?
Less able: Provide the children with adult help to remember or record where they found the plants they drew, and to decide where to stick their drawings on the class plan.

Links to other topics
Art: Making collages using plant materials. Remind the children to take only very small samples of plants, or to use dead materials.

HERE AND THERE

Where is it?

- Find the yellow beanbag.
- Draw something that is **under** it.

- Find the blue beanbag.
- Draw something that is **far away from** it.

- Find the green beanbag.
- Draw something that is **next to it**.

- Find the red beanbag.
- Draw something that it is **on**.

NOW TRY THIS

On the back of this sheet, draw and colour one of the balls. Write position labels to show where it is.

Where is it?

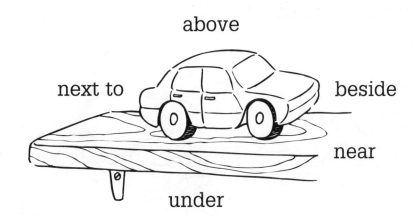

above

next to

beside

near

under

far away

■ Look around your classroom. Draw what you can see:

under the yellow beanbag

next to the green beanbag

■ Draw arrows from the labels to things in the picture.

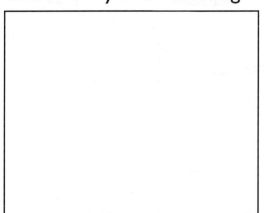

Under the table.

On the table.

Beside the table.

SHAPE AND SPACE
PHOTOCOPIABLE

Find the treasure

Here is a map of Pirate island.

What is above the rocks? _____

▨ A bear is inside the cave. Draw the bear.

▨ A monkey is beside the tree. Draw the monkey.

▨ Follow these instructions to find the treasure.

Start at the tree. Follow the path. Turn away
from the ship. Keep following the path.

Where is the treasure hidden? _____

Where do they grow?

Where did you find plants?
- Draw or describe some places.

- Draw one plant carefully.

Where was this plant growing?

_____

_____

Did anyone else find the same type of plant?

_____

Where was their plant growing?

_____

_____

WRITE A LIST

MATHS FOCUS: MAKING LISTS

Learning objectives
■ To understand and use the words *sort, list, count* in practical contexts.
■ To make and organise lists.

Resources
■ A selection of familiar classroom objects used for writing, drawing, counting and maths, a flip chart or board, marker pens, pencils, Blu-Tack, scissors, old magazines and catalogues.
■ Photocopiable pages 48 (page 49 for less able children) and 50 for each child.

Introduction
5 mins
■ Explain that this lesson is about sorting things out and making lists. Ask the children when they have to sort things into groups – for example, toys to give away and toys to keep, or things that belong in the bedroom and things that belong downstairs. Talk about times when they might make lists: friends to invite to a party, shopping, things to do at home.

Whole-class, teacher-directed activity
10–15 mins
■ Display a selection of classroom objects. Ask: *How could we sort these out?* Prompt the children to think about what they use the objects for. After discussion, make three labels: 'drawing', 'counting or sums' and 'writing'.
■ Divide the flip chart or board into three columns and stick one of the labels at the top of the left-hand column. *Which objects belong with this label?* Use Blu-Tack to fasten the correct objects under the heading. Repeat with the other labels and objects.
■ Show the children how to make a list by replacing each of the objects with its written name.

Children's activity
15–20 mins
■ The children can complete photocopiable page 48. They need to decide which person the various items belong to, and make a list for each person showing their belongings. While some objects are easy to sort, others could be included in more than one list. Encourage the children to discuss which objects might be used by more than one group of people – for instance, both a toddler and a Year 1 child might use building blocks.
■ The children can then cut out pictures of objects from magazines or catalogues and sort them in appropriate ways (see 'Differentiation').

Differentiation
More able: The children can sort magazine pictures of toys into two or three groups of their own choice (such as *indoor toys* and *outdoor toys* or *loud toys* and *quiet toys*).

Less able: The children can use photocopiable page 49 and old catalogues to cut out pictures of things suitable for different people and stick them down in the boxes on the sheet. With help, they can make lists of these objects.

SCIENCE LINK ACTIVITY

Photocopiable page 50 gives children more practice in sorting items and making lists. The children sort and make lists of a range of objects associated with water use. The objects can be grouped according to what they are used for; what they are made from; whether they use clean or dirty water; whether they use a lot of water or a little water; whether they are used indoors or outdoors; or another grouping of the children's own choice.

Plenary
10 mins
■ Share some of the children's lists. Demonstrate that it does not matter what order the listed items are in. Look at some of the magazine pictures the children have sorted. Do the other children think these were put into the correct groups? Talk about other places where lists are used (school registers, lists of children in reading groups, ice cream flavours and so on).

MATHS SKILLS FOR SCIENCE: YEARS I&2

SCIENCE FOCUS: USING WATER (QCA UNIT IC, SCOTTISH GUIDELINES LEVEL A)

Learning objectives
- To recognise water as a common material.
- To know that water is used for many purposes.
- To identify different uses of water.

Resources
- Examples of objects associated with water use (such as a small watering can, tumbler, soap, toothbrush).
- Pictures of people using water in various ways.
- A flip chart or board, Blu-Tack.
- A copy of photocopiable page 51 for each child .

Introduction
5–10 mins
- Show the children a range of objects associated with using water. *How can we sort these objects?* Discuss the children's ideas. They may well sort the objects according to what material they are made from. Prompt them to think about water, the material that connects all the different objects. *Where do we find water? What can we use it for?* Discuss some of the different ways the children use water.

Whole-class, teacher-directed activity
5–10 mins
- Explain that, just as materials such as metal and wood are used for lots of different things, we can use water in lots of ways. Write some of the ways that water can be used – for example, drinking, washing and playing – as headings across the top of the board.
- Help the children to group the pictures of people using water under the correct headings, and then to write lists. Encourage them to think about some less familiar uses of water. Children of this age often do not realise that fruit drinks, soups and bubble-blowing mixtures, for example, are mostly water. Mixing up examples of these to be sorted helps to emphasise the use of water in them.

Children's activity
20–25 mins
- Working in pairs or small groups, the children can carry out a 'water survey' around the school. They can find and record (by drawing or writing on a copy of photocopiable page 51) as many ways as possible in which water is being used. They can decide how to group the different water uses, and make a list under each heading they have. They could use the groups discussed in the class activity, or choose their own.

Differentiation
More able: Challenge the children to work together to think of people who use water in their jobs, and to describe what they use it for. Examples might include firefighters putting out fires, nurses bathing wounds, cooks cooking food, cleaners washing floors. Each child should draw a picture to illustrate someone using water at work.
Less able: Ask the children to collect objects associated with water use, such as paintbrushes, paper towels, cups and so on. Give them two or three types of water use, such as *drinking*, *playing* and possibly *cleaning*, to use as headings for lists. Help them to decide which list each of their objects belongs in.

Links to other topics
Citizenship: Water safety – ways to play safely on the beach, at the swimming pool, in paddling pools and so on.
Art: Painting with watery paints or very thick paints. Making swirly water-pattern pictures (marbling), flour paste pictures, batik (wax and water paint) pictures.
Geography: A water tour (real or using videos) to see where water occurs naturally – seas, rivers, lakes, ponds.

WRITE A LIST

Who is this for?

■ Look at these things. Who could they belong to?

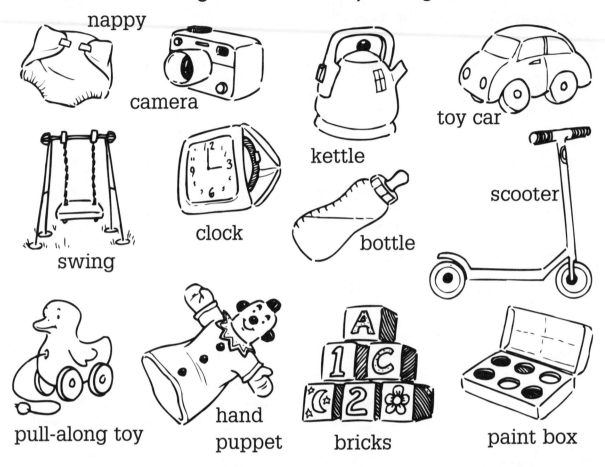

nappy

camera

kettle

toy car

swing

clock

bottle

scooter

pull-along toy

hand puppet

bricks

paint box

■ Write the names of the things in lists.

Baby	Toddler	Year 1 boy or girl	Grown-up
	toy car		

NOW TRY THIS Look at pictures of toys. Sort them into two or three groups. Write lists of them on the back of this sheet.

Who needs this?

■ Cut out and stick down pictures, or draw your own, to show things each person might need.

Baby	Year 1 child	Grown-up

■ Use your groups of things to write lists.

Baby
Year 1 child
Grown-up

WRITE A LIST

Using water

All these things are used with water.

mug	teapot	straw
bath	boat	swim ring
water tray	bird bath	watering can
bubbles	dog dish	bucket

■ Cut out the pictures.
■ Sort them into groups.
■ Use your groups to write lists.

WRITE A LIST

Water survey

▧ Draw or write about the ways of using water you have found.

▧ Sort out your ways of using water.
▧ Choose three of these groups:

drinking   washing   gardening
pets   playing   working

▧ Make lists of the three groups.

On the back of this sheet, draw someone who uses water in his or her job.

FIND THE FACTS

RECORDING AND ORGANISING DATA

MATHS FOCUS: MAKING LISTS AND TWO-COLUMN TABLES

Learning objectives
- To make a list.
- To collect data and make a two-column table.

Resources
- Examples of clothing worn for different purposes (scarf, helmet, gardening gloves, plastic apron, sunhat, Wellington boots and so on), a flip chart or board.
- Catalogues or magazines with pictures showing different types of clothing (uniforms, protective clothing, sports clothing and so on), scissors, adhesive, plain A4 paper.
- Photocopiable pages 54 (page 55 for less able children) and 56.

Introduction
Up to 5 mins
- Talk about different types of clothing worn for different purposes. *Are there any times when you wear special clothing?* (Party clothes, school uniform, painting clothes.) *Do you know any other people who wear special clothing?* (People who wear uniforms, protective clothing such as helmets or overalls, sports clothing.)

Whole-class, teacher-directed activity
5–10 mins
- Show the children the examples of clothing. Talk about what these are, who might wear them, when and for what purpose. Make a list of the names of these types of clothing.
- Ask: *How could we tell someone more about these clothes? How could we write down who wears them, or what the clothes are used for, in a way that is really easy to read?* Explain that tables allow us to show a lot of information in a form that can easily be read. Give examples, such as a table of children's names and hair colours.
- Draw lines around and across your list of clothes to make it into a two-column table. Use the second column to show either who wears the clothes or what they are used for.

Children's activity
20–25 mins
- Ask the children to cut out pictures of 'special' clothes from catalogues or magazines. Using A4 paper and adhesive, they can make composite (photofit) pictures of people wearing various articles of 'special' clothing. They can use a copy of photocopiable page 54 to list the types of clothing their person is wearing, then fill in the table by writing the purpose of each type of clothing (for example, keeping warm).

Differentiation
More able: The children can use catalogues or magazines to find examples of as many different ways of using clothes as possible. Examples could include showing what a person docs (uniform), protection (overalls), safety (helmet), keeping warm, keeping cool and so on.
Less able: The children can use the outline person on photocopiable page 55 to help them organise enough items of clothing for one person. They can list the items of clothing used by name on the sheet.

SCIENCE LINK ACTIVITY

Photocopiable page 56 shows a variety of different types of lights, many of which will be familiar to the children. The children are asked to make three different lists, showing lights that are used for different purposes. For one of their lists, they have to make a table including information about who might use each light.

Plenary
10 mins
- Look at some of the children's photofit people. Ask some children to describe what their tables show (for example: 'We found three things to keep you warm and one thing to protect you'). Recap on what a list is: a set of things that all have something in common. Remind the children that a table is like a list, but it gives more information about each item in the list.

SCIENCE FOCUS: LIGHT AND DARK (QCA UNIT 1D)

Learning objectives
- To know that there are many sources of light.
- To observe and make comparisons between sources of light.

Resources
- Some examples of light sources (such as a candle, torch, desk lamp, Christmas tree lights).
- Posters or pictures showing lights (night-time street scenes, the Moon and stars, firework displays, bonfires, religious celebrations such as Christmas and Divali), a wipe-clean clipboard or memo board, a marker pen. Different-coloured torches and stubby candles, a tray, sand, pieces of coloured transparent plastic.
- A copy per child of photocopiable page 57.

Introduction
5 mins
- Ask the children to share their experiences of different kinds of lights. (Some children may not have experienced lighted streets or stars.) Discuss lights that are used for different purposes: to help us see in the dark (streetlights, torches), for visual effect (birthday candles, fireworks, religious celebrations), for warning (red or blue danger lights), for information (traffic lights, on/off lights). Discuss the meanings of some coloured lights: blue lights on vehicles are emergency lights; red lights mean 'Stop' and green lights mean 'Safe to go'.

Whole-class, teacher-directed activity
10–15 mins
- Look at examples of light sources. *What are these used for?* Start a class list of light sources.
- Take the children on a 'light walk' around the school. Find as many different light sources as possible, making a class list on a wipe-clean clipboard or memo board. Discuss what each light source is for: helping us to see, warning, information, fun and so on.
- In the classroom, show the children the pictures or posters of lights. Help them to identify lights for different purposes and make lists on the board.
- Discuss how the lights differ from each other. Look for lights that are bright or dim, white or coloured and so on.
- Show the children some coloured light sources, such as different-coloured torches and candles. Ask them what colour the light will be. A few children may think that coloured candles give coloured light. Demonstrate that they do not. (For safety, use stubby candles in a metal tray filled with sand. Do not allow children near the flames.) Look at the white light of a torch. Show that this can be turned into coloured light by putting pieces of coloured transparent plastic in front of the torch.

Children's activity
20–25 mins
- In pairs, the children can use photocopiable page 57 to make a list of lights that are used for celebrations or for fun. Examples may include birthday cake candles, sparklers, Christmas tree lights, torches and toy lights. They can use pictures, posters or their own knowledge. Write a selection of the children's ideas on the board in the form of a two-column table, with the type of light in the left-hand column and the colour of the light in the right-hand column.

Differentiation
More able: Can the children think of any more lights that are coloured? What colours are they? Do they know what different colours mean – in traffic lights, for example?
Less able: The children can make a list of lights on page 57, but not complete the table.

Links to other topics
PSHE/citizenship: The meaning of warning or information lights in different circumstances, such as red/green man at pelican crossings and blue flashing lights on emergency vehicles.
Art: Make collage pictures showing a variety of light sources, such as firework displays.
Literacy: Read stories about the effects of light and darkness, such as *The Owl Who Was Afraid Of the Dark* by Jill Tomlinson or *The Train Who Was Frightened Of the Dark* by Denis Bond.

RECORDING AND ORGANISING DATA
PHOTOCOPIABLE

Special clothing

■ Look at the picture you have made of a person wearing different kinds of special clothes. In the box below, list the clothes your person is wearing.

■ Fill in this table to show what the different clothes are for.

Clothing	What it is for

Special clothing

Can you dress up this person? Cut out pictures of different kinds of special clothing and stick them on this picture.

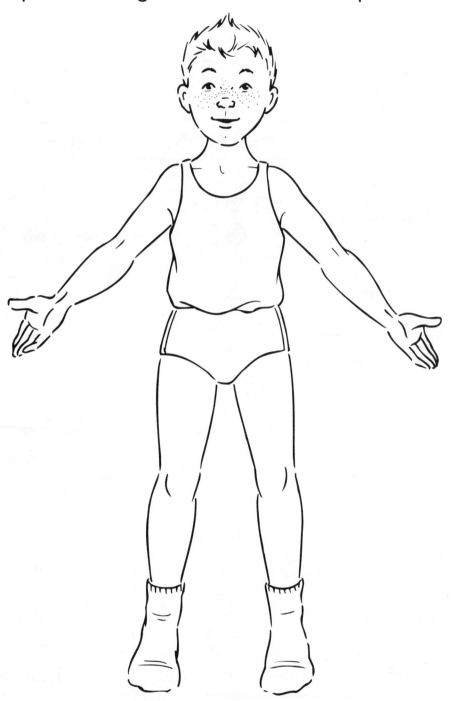

List your person's special clothing here.

Lots of lights

Here are some different lights.

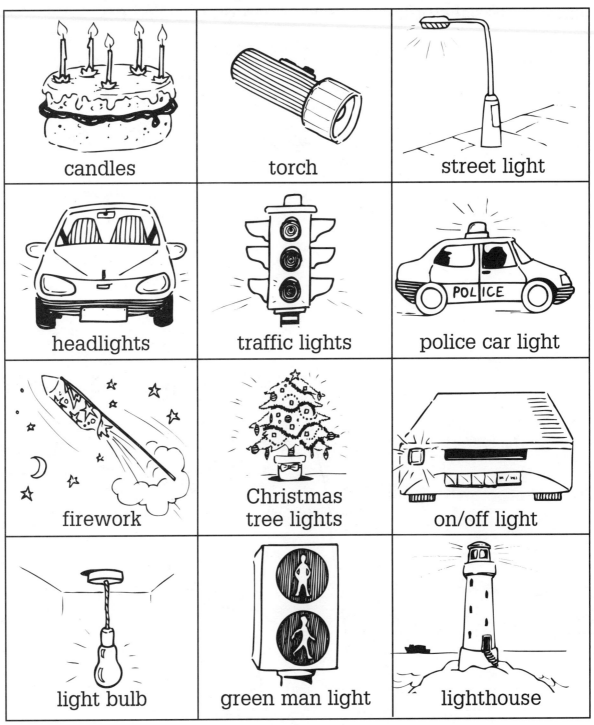

candles | torch | street light

headlights | traffic lights | police car light

firework | Christmas tree lights | on/off light

light bulb | green man light | lighthouse

■ What are the lights for? Sort them by making three lists:

For fun   To see with   To tell us things

■ Choose one list. Make a table to say who uses each light.

Light   Who uses it?

RECORDING AND ORGANISING DATA

PHOTOCOPIABLE

A list of lights

■ Write some things that we use lights for.

Helping us see.

■ Think of some lights that are used for fun or celebration.
■ Make a list of them.

What colour are these lights?
■ Make a table.

Type of light	Colour

NOW TRY THIS Can you think of any more coloured lights?
Talk to your teacher about what they are used for.

SPOT THE DIFFERENCES

MATHS FOCUS: REPRESENTING INFORMATION AS PICTURE CHARTS

Learning objectives
- To sort objects or pictures into sets.
- To represent information about sorting by making a 'picture graph' using objects or pictures.
- To use a 'picture graph' to count the number of objects in a set.

Resources
- A selection of pencils, sharpeners and rubbers (with a total of 20 or less).
- A large picture from a poster, large magazine or calendar (to cut up) showing a range of images including people (such as a street, farmyard or park scene).
- Old magazines, scissors, adhesive, Blu-Tack, a board or flip chart and marker pens.
- An A3 copy of photocopiable page 60 (page 61 for less able children) for each group. An A4 copy of photocopiable page 62 for each child.

Introduction
5 mins
- Show the children the selection of pencils, sharpeners and rubbers. Ask: *Who can sort these out for me?* Ask a volunteer to sort them, then explain what groups he or she has made: 'I put all the pencils together.'
- Write the labels 'pencil', 'sharpener' and 'rubber' across the bottom of the board or flip chart, then use Blu-Tack to stick the objects in three columns. Count how many there are of each object. Ask: *How many things are there altogether?*

Whole-class, teacher-directed activity
5–10 mins
- Show the children the large picture. Discuss what things can be seen in it. Decide how some of them could be grouped: *people, toys, plants* and so on. Choose three or four of these groups and write them across the bottom of the board or flip chart.
- Point out that you can't stick the real objects onto the picture graph this time. Ask the children to suggest another way to show the groups.
- Make a picture graph with cut-out pictures of appropriate objects in each labelled column. Again, count how many items are in each group and how many there are altogether.

Children's activity
20–25 mins
- Working in groups, the children can find and cut out magazine pictures to go into each of the sets provided on photocopiable page 60. They can stick these in the appropriate places on an A3 copy of the worksheet to make their own group picture graph.

Differentiation
More able: Ask the children to write sentences to describe their picture graphs, such as: 'We found 6 pictures of food.' 'There were more pictures of people than of anything else.' 'We found 16 pictures altogether.'

Less able: The children can use photocopiable page 61 to sort pictures into two sets: *people* and *not people*. Provide help as necessary with cutting out and placing the pictures.

SCIENCE LINK ACTIVITY

The children can use photocopiable page 62 to consider ways in which children can differ. They should colour the pictures of two children to match the descriptions given, then sort other descriptive words by matching them to the correct picture.

Plenary
10 mins
- Display some of the children's picture graphs. Ask: *Are they all the same?* Encourage the children to discuss ways in which the picture graphs differ, concentrating on overall information rather than individual pictures. For example, encourage statements such as 'They found more pictures of food than our group' rather than 'They found a picture of a tomato and we didn't.'

SPOT THE DIFFERENCES

SCIENCE FOCUS: OURSELVES (QCA UNIT 1A)

Learning objectives
- To be aware that there are differences between humans.
- To collect information and present it in a picture graph.

Resources
- Unbreakable hand-held mirrors, coloured pencils.
- Large magazine pictures of two people who are clearly different (male and female, dark and fair hair, tall and short and so on).
- A3 sheets of paper (these could be labelled beforehand) to make group picture graphs, scissors, adhesive.
- A copy of photocopiable page 63 for each child.

Introduction
5 mins
- Show the children the two magazine pictures. Ask them to spot as many differences as they can. Make a list of the differences. Concentrate on characteristics that are not easily changed, such as eye colour, hair colour and hair type (straight or wavy). In later school work, these characteristics will be used to examine inherited differences between people. Explain the difference between these features and features such as jumper colour and hair length, which can easily be changed from day to day.

Whole-class, teacher-directed activity
10 mins
- Give the children hand-held mirrors (one each, or one per pair or small group). Ask them to observe themselves closely, looking at things like eye colour, hair colour and hair type. Discuss some of the ways in which children in the class differ from each other in their appearance. Stress that we are all unique, all individuals and all important, but that we can sort people into sets or groups with similar characteristics, and that doing this can help us to understand the similarities and differences between people.
- Choose a characteristic such as eye colour. Ask: *What sets could we use to sort children with different eye colours?* Help the children to decide on appropriate sets (blue, brown, perhaps grey or green). Label a picture graph with an appropriate title and sets.
- Choose a different characteristic: either hair colour or hair type, but not both. Again, help the children to decide on appropriate sets and label a picture graph accordingly. Make an appropriately labelled picture graph sheet for each group (these can be done beforehand and given to the children, provided that you lead the class discussion to the characteristics and sets you have already chosen).
- As an alternative, the children could make one large class picture graph for eye colour and another for hair colour or hair type.

Children's activity
20–25 mins
- The children can use copies of photocopiable page 63 to record, in picture form, their own eye colour and hair colour or type. They can then cut out these pictures and stick them on their group (or class) picture graph sheets to make one picture graph for eye colour and a second for either hair colour or hair type.

Differentiation
More able: Ask the children to use their picture graph sheets to find out which is the most common eye colour and the most common hair colour or type in their group. Do they think the answer would be the same for groups in other classes, schools or countries?
Less able: The children can make just one picture graph, grouping themselves according to eye colour. The eye colours can be grouped as just 'blue' or 'brown'.

Links to other topics
PSHE/citizenship: Valuing each other's differences – in culture, not just in appearance.
Art: Making accurate paintings, collages or models of ourselves.

SPOT THE DIFFERENCES

Making a picture graph

☐ Cut out magazine pictures.
☐ Stick them here to make a picture graph.

Magazine pictures			
People	Food	Plants	Other

☐ Write a sentence about your picture graph.

_____

_____

HANDLING AND INTERPRETING DATA

PHOTOCOPIABLE

Making a picture graph

- Cut out magazine pictures.
- Stick them here to make a picture graph.

Magazine pictures	
People	Not people

Spot the differences

■ Colour these children's eyes and hair.
Use the words on the picture to help you.

Blue eyes
Fair hair

Brown eyes
Brown hair

■ Read the labels below. Which child does each label describe?
■ Write each label next to the correct child.

Tall	Wavy hair	Small hands
Short	Straight hair	Big hands

What are you like?

▪ Draw your eyes in this box.
▪ Colour them.

▪ Write a label for your drawing. Use one of these words:

blue	brown	grey	green

▪ Draw your hair
in this box.
▪ Colour it.

▪ Write a label
for your drawing.
Use one of these
words. You can use
more than one
word if you like.

curly
wavy
straight
brown
fair
black

**NOW
TRY
THIS**   What is the most common eye colour in your group?

SORTING MATERIALS

MATHS FOCUS: REPRESENTING INFORMATION IN PICTOGRAMS

Learning objectives
- To collect information by sorting.
- To represent information by drawing and correctly placing pictures.

Resources
- A jar of different-shaped buttons (square, circle, triangle, star), A3 plain paper, marker pens, Blu-Tack.
- A selection of small objects (such as blocks, cotton reels or buttons) in four colours, 'feely' bags, small trays, squares of plain paper (5cm × 5cm), coloured pencils, adhesive.
- Photocopiable pages 66 (page 67 for less able children), 68 and resource page 125 for each child.

Introduction
Up to 5 mins
- Discuss examples of sorting: mixed-up pieces for games or jigsaws, different colours or types of washing, sharing assorted sweets fairly. Ask questions such as: *Why do we sometimes count things we have sorted? Are all the jigsaw pieces there? Who has the most orange Smarties? How many toy aeroplanes have you collected?*
- Explain that a pictogram is a special way of recording how objects have been sorted, so that you can count them easily.

Whole-class, teacher-directed activity
5–10 mins
- Display a jar of different-shaped buttons. *What shapes are there?* Draw the shapes and write their names along the bottom of a sheet of A3 paper.
- Ask each child to take one button at random from the jar. Ask them in turn to identify their shape; use Blu-Tack to stick each button above the correct label on the sheet.
- Use this pictogram to count the number of circle or square buttons chosen. *How many children were there altogether? Which shape did the most/least children pick?*
- Display the pictogram.

Children's activity
20–25 mins
- Give each group a plastic tray, squares of paper and a 'feely' bag containing small objects in different colours. The children select an object from the bag in turn, draw and colour it on a paper square, then put the object in the tray. They continue until the 'feely' bag is empty.
  - They draw coloured labels across the bottom of a sheet of A3 paper, then stick their pictures above the correct labels to form a pictogram. Photocopiable page 60 provides instructions for this task and questions to follow it.

SCIENCE LINK ACTIVITY

The children can cut out the pictures from page 68 and make a pictogram by sticking them onto a copy of resource page 125. They should group the objects according to what they are made from. Compare the children's pictograms. Discuss why the children thought some objects were made from different materials. Sometimes we cannot tell from a picture, and have to use other senses: how things sound or feel.

Differentiation
More able: The children can make up more questions like those on page 66 for other children in the group to answer.
Less able: Give the children an A3 copy of the labelled pictogram on photocopiable page 67 to stick their drawings onto. Limit the total number of objects to ten or less. You could limit the number of colours to three, or even two.

Plenary
10 mins
- Look at some of the children's pictograms. Ask the class: *Are the pictures in the correct places?* Answer the questions from page 66. Help the children to think of similar questions and find the answers.

SCIENCE FOCUS: SORTING MATERIALS (QCA UNIT 1C)

Learning objectives
- To be aware that materials have properties that we can recognise using our senses.
- To identify the properties of different materials.

Resources
- Examples of objects made from materials that are hard, soft, smooth, rough, shiny, dull and so on, a 'feely' bag.
- A copy of photocopiable page 69 and resource page 125 for each group.

Introduction
Up to 5 mins
- Show the children some examples of objects with different properties. Check that they understand the appropriate vocabulary. *Can you see an object that is hard? Tell the other children what this object is like.* Encourage them to use a wide range of vocabulary to describe the objects.

Whole-class, teacher-directed activity
10 mins
- Ask a volunteer to hold an object in a 'feely' bag and to describe it, using as many describing words as he or she can for its properties. The other children can try to identify the object from its description.
- Ask the volunteer to hold up the object. *Did you guess what it was? Did Emily describe it correctly?* Allow several children to describe objects in this way.
- As a variation, you could ask a blindfolded child to describe objects given to him or her by other children. The other children should ask questions that prompt the blindfolded child to use all of his or her senses: *What does it smell like? Does it make a noise? Is it hard or soft?*

Children's activity
20–25 mins
- Working in small groups, the children can choose four or five different properties and then look for objects with these properties. They can use copies of photocopiable page 69 and resource page 125 (either at A4 size or enlarged to A3) to record these objects and make a pictogram: first they draw the objects and label them with their properities, then they cut out the labelled pictures and stick them onto page 125. The children in the group should all agree on the property of the object – for example, if one of the listed properties is 'hard', an object should only be included in the pictogram if all the children in the group agree that the object is hard.
- Discuss with the children what properties are needed in materials to make particular objects. *Would you make a chair from something bendy? What would you use? Why would you choose that material?*

Differentiation
More able: Encourage the children to use more than one property to describe the objects they find. For example, a wooden spoon is 'hard' and 'dull'. They should put the object on their pictogram in the column that they think describes its most important property.
Less able: Help the children to choose just two or three properties to look for. Give them a selection of objects to choose from, each of which has one of the properties chosen.

Links to other topics
Ourselves: Thinking about our five senses. Which senses do the children use the most?
History: Looking at pictures of old-fashioned objects, such as toys, school benches or chairs. *What were they made from? How have they changed? Do you like the changes? Why do you think they might have changed?*
Music/Drama: Choosing the correct materials to make the right sounds for a particular mood, or sound effects for plays. *What makes a good noise for horses' hooves? For rain?*

SORTING MATERIALS

What colour are they?

■ Do these things.

1. Take an object.

2. Draw and colour it.

3. Put the object in a tray.

■ Use your small pictures to make a pictogram, like this:

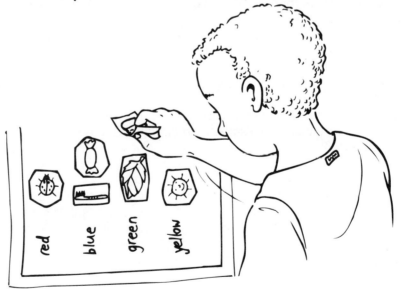

How many objects were there altogether? _____

How many of the objects were red? _____

What was the colour of the largest group of objects? _____

Pictogram of coloured objects

How many?

red　　　　blue　　　　green　　　　yellow

SORTING MATERIALS

What are they made from?

Here are some objects made from metal, plastic or wood.

spoon	pencil	toy car
pencil sharpener	knife	toy bricks
mug	pair of scissors	door
ruler	table	bowl

Cut out the pictures. Make a pictogram to show what the objects are made from.

NOW TRY THIS Is it easy to tell what the objects are made from?

SORTING MATERIALS

How can we describe it?

What properties are you going to look for?
▢ Circle some from this list, or choose your own.

hard   soft   shiny   dull   rough   smooth

Find some objects. What are their properties?
▢ Draw the objects here. Under each picture, write the properties.

▢ Make a pictogram to show what properties the objects have.
Use the pictogram worksheet for this.

NOW TRY THIS Can you use two or more words to describe some of your objects?

KEEPING A TALLY

MATHS FOCUS: MAKING TALLY CHARTS

Learning objectives
- To record things by keeping a tally.
- To count in steps of 5.

Resources
- A flip chart or board and marker pens, a selection of objects to tally, such as coloured beads, sweets or toy farmyard animals.
- A large container for each group, a small pot or tray for each child.
- Photocopiable pages 72, 73, 74 and 127 for each child.

Introduction
Up to 5 mins
- Explain that sometimes when we count, we can't start again if we lose count – for example, counting goals our team has scored. Can the children think of more examples? Explain that tally charts let us 'count as we go along', without having to remember the number.

Whole-class, teacher-directed activity
10 mins
- Show the children how to make a tally chart by drawing a vertical line for every 'one' that they count. Every fifth line is a diagonal going through the other four, making a group of five. Show the children your selection of objects, one at a time, asking them to keep a tally on resource page 127 of one type of object (such as the red beads or the toy sheep). Ask them to count up the total on their tally charts.
- Draw a tally chart like that on page 72 on the board. Ask four volunteers to tally different types of object (for example, red beads, blue beads, green beads and yellow beads) as you show them a selection of objects, one at a time. Help them to work out the totals from their tally charts. Check by counting the number of each type of object in the pile on the table.
- Repeat, with different children doing the tallying.

Children's activity
20 mins
- Place a large container of assorted objects in the centre of each group. Give each child a small tray or container and a copy of page 72, with the appropriate 'tallying groups' labelled.
- The children should work individually, taking objects from the central container one at a time, making a tally mark in the correct part of their chart, then putting the object in their own container or tray. They should continue until their own tray is full, then work out the totals from their tally chart and check by counting the objects in their tray.

Differentiation
More able: The children can use smaller objects, so their totals are larger. Suggest other things they could count by tallying, such as children with pets or children with their own pencil case. If possible, let them try out their ideas.
Less able: Give the children larger-sized objects, so the totals on their tally chart and in their trays are smaller.

SCIENCE LINK ACTIVITY

Photocopiable page 73 shows a picture of all the different minibeasts found by an imaginary class. The children can use this to make a tally chart. Discuss with them how to tally the minibeasts. Page 74 suggests one possible set of headings for the tally chart. You may prefer to allow some groups of children to choose their own headings, possibly using animal names such as those on photocopiable page 74.

Plenary
10 mins
- Look at some individual tally charts. Ask: *What objects did you have most of?* Ask the children to explain how they found this out from their tally charts. Discuss other things they might be able to count using tally charts.

SCIENCE FOCUS: LIVING THINGS IN THE LOCAL ENVIRONMENT (QCA UNIT 2B)

Learning objectives

- To know that there are different kinds of plants and animals in the immediate environment.
- To observe animals and plants found and record them in a tally chart.
- To know that there are differences between local habitats.

Resources

- Access to several different types of habitat (such as paved, grassy, hedgerow and flowerbed areas).
- Simple books, with large clear pictures, about plants and minibeasts to help with identification, writing and drawing materials, blank paper.
- A copy of photocopiable page 74 or 75 for each child.

Preparation: Consult your school's policy on fieldwork. Make sure there will be adequate supervision of non-classroom activities. If necessary, place stones, plant pots and so on (for minibeasts to hide under) a few days before this activity.

Introduction

10–15 mins

- Ask: *What living things are there around our school? Where do you think we might find them?* Encourage the children to think about outdoors as well as indoors! You may need to prompt them to think of tiny 'creepy-crawlies' as well as larger creatures. Many children at this age may not remember that plants are also living things.
- Remind the children that living things can be divided into two groups: plants and animals. Can they name any plants or animals that might live around the school? Make lists under the headings 'Plants' and 'Animals', together with the children's suggestions about where these might be found.
- Remind the children about recording information in tally charts, and check that they all remember how to make a tally chart.
- Talk to the children about caring for other living things and their environment. Explain why they should not pick up or move the minibeasts they find, or pull up or break plants, and why they should put all stones, plant pots and so on back where they found them. Explain any safety rules about where they can and cannot go to look for plants or minibeasts. Make sure they all understand why it is important to wash their hands after touching soil or plants.

Children's activity

20–25 mins

- Decide as a class whether to search for plants or minibeasts, and discuss what sort of places might have a lot of plants or minibeasts.
- Assign each small group of children to a different part of the school grounds, or to a different type of area (paved, grassy and so on). They should spend 10–15 minutes searching their area and recording what they find in drawings (on blank paper) and on photocopiable page 74 (minibeasts) or 75 (plants).
- Make sure the children understand that the class will be comparing the numbers of living things found in different areas to see whether their original ideas were correct. If there do not seem to be many plants or animals in their area, they must record what they find and not move to a 'better' area.

Differentiation

This activity should be accessible to all the children, working in mixed-ability groups. Provide differentiation through the different-level reference books (or other sources) the children use.

Links to other topics

Literacy/Art: Imaginative writing or simple shape poems about real or imaginary minibeasts; collages or models to show these.

Citizenship: Care for the environment. Local wildlife groups may be able to supply experts to talk to the children.

KEEPING A TALLY

Making tally charts

■ Tally your objects.

Take an object.   Draw a tally mark.   Put the object in
your tray.

My tally chart

	Total
	Total
	Total
	Total

NOW TRY THIS What other things could you count by tallying?

Class 2's minibeast hunt

Here are all the minibeasts that the children in Class 2 found.

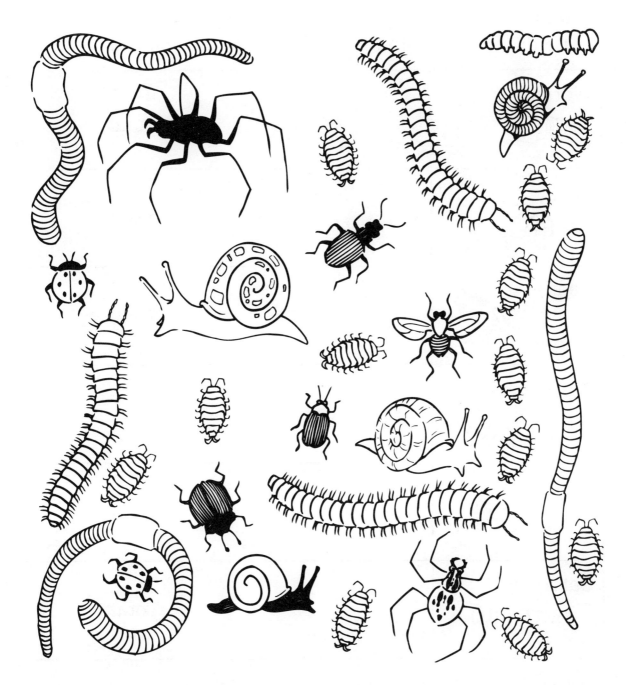

■ On another sheet of paper, make a tally chart using these labels:

wings	no legs	6 legs	lots of legs

■ Write the total for each group on the tally chart.

How many minibeasts did Class 2 find altogether? _____

Our minibeast hunt

Where are you going to look for minibeasts?
How many minibeasts do you think you will find?

Use this tally chart to record the minibeasts you find.

Worm	Total
Snail	Total
Beetle	Total
Woodlouse	Total
Spider	Total
Caterpillar	Total
Other	Total

What types of area do most minibeasts live in?

_____

_____

Our plant hunt

Where are you going to look for plants?

How many plants do you think you will find?

Use this tally chart to record the plants you find.

Daisy	Total
Dandelion	Total
Buttercup	Total
Nettle	Total
Bramble	Total
Tree or bush	Total
Garden plants	Total

What types of area had lots of plants?

What types of area had very few plants?

SEE THE PATTERN

MATHS FOCUS: RECOGNISING PATTERNS AND RELATIONSHIPS

Learning objectives
- To recognise a simple relationship between length and number.
- To recognise a simple doubling pattern.
- To make predictions about the next term in a series.

Resources
- Pencils, paper, scissors, Blu-Tack, counters, beads, blocks.
- Different-sized containers for the extension activity (such as 250g, 500g and 1kg margarine tubs from the same brand of margarine).
- Photocopiable pages 78 (page 79 for more able children) and 80.

Introduction
10 mins
- Have a 'question and answer' session on building and identifying patterns: *This is an 'add on 2' pattern – join in when you can: 2, 4, 6, 8...* Build addition and subtraction patterns. Say the numbers in a pattern and ask the children to identify it (for example, 'take away 2').

Whole-class, teacher-directed activity
10 mins
- Fasten a strip of paper the exact length of 3 blocks on the board. Ask a child to fasten as many blocks as possible to it, using Blu-Tack. *How many has s/he fitted on?* Fasten another strip of paper twice as long as the first on the board. *How many blocks can we fit on this strip?* Repeat for strips three and four times as long as the original strip. Each time, ask the children to predict the number of blocks and then to check.
- Use blocks to make other patterns, such as *add three* or *add four*. Extend this to patterns involving simple doubling and halving.
- Fold or cut large sheets of coloured paper to make patterns, such as: fold lengthwise, widthwise, then lengthwise. Can they predict what will happen next?
- **Extension:** What happens to the size of the paper when it is folded?

Children's activity
20–25 mins
- The children can use photocopiable page 78 to practise spotting a relationship between the length of a 'scarf' and the number of letters or objects that will fit along it.
- They can use blocks to make up patterns, drawing and describing them on page 78.

Differentiation
More able: The children can use photocopiable page 79 to practise seeing and making a three-dimensional pattern (the number of blocks that fit in a container) that involves a doubling in size from one step to the next.

Less able: The children can use real paper strips in the same proportion as the strips on photocopiable page 78: 10cm, 20cm, 30cm and 40cm. Ask the children to make a pattern by sticking identical real objects (such as buttons, beads or blocks) onto the strips using Blu-Tack. Explain how the pattern develops: *When the strip gets longer, I can put more blocks on it.* Can the children make a rough estimate of how many blocks will fit on the next length?

SCIENCE LINK ACTIVITY

Photocopiable page 80 shows four teddy bears of increasing size. It asks the children to spot the relationships between different lengths in a teddy bear design, and to make predictions: 'As the teddies get taller, their legs get longer. I predict that the tallest teddy will have the longest legs.'

Plenary
10 mins
- Ask the children to describe the pattern shown on page 78. Some may say 'There are more letters when the scarf is longer'; others may give more detail, saying 'It is going up 5 every time.' Ask the children to share and describe some of the patterns they have created.

SCIENCE FOCUS: VARIATION (QCA UNIT 2C)

Learning objectives
- To explore human variation, making observations and comparisons.
- To make predictions about differences between themselves, test them and decide whether they were correct.

Resources
- Tape measures, metre rulers, clocks with a loud tick.
- Two copies of photocopiable page 81 and a copy of resource page 126 for each child.

Introduction
5 mins
- Discuss ways in which the children are similar or different in their physical features. Move from simple comparisons (we all have two arms) to comparisons involving measurement (our legs are always longer than our arms, different people have different arm lengths).

Whole-class, teacher-directed activity
10–15 mins
- Make a prediction, such as: *The older children in this class are taller than the younger children.* Invite the children to suggest ways to test your prediction. Prompt them to think about questions such as: *What will we have to measure? What will we measure it with? How will we record our results?*
- Test the prediction by lining the children up in age order. Use direct comparison or measurement to see whether the older children are generally taller. Ask the children to decide whether the original prediction was correct. (It does not matter that the data will probably not support their prediction, because the age range is too small.)
- Ask: *What other things could we test?* (Do children with longer arms have larger hands? Do the children with the longest legs run the fastest?) Help the children to change their question into a prediction: *We predict that the children with the longest legs also have the longest arms.* Decide on a class prediction to investigate.

Children's activity
20–25 mins
- Working in groups of up to six, the children should decide what they need to measure in order to test the class prediction. They can use a copy of photocopiable page 81 to record the prediction and the results in table form.
- They rearrange the entries in their table (using a second copy of page 126) so that the entries in the left-hand column are in ascending order, the smallest first. (Make sure the children understand that in the example given, the values for Fiona's leg length and her jump distance must stay on the same row.) If there is a direct connection between the value being looked at (such as length of leg) and the value being measured (such as the distance the child can jump), the values in the right-hand column should also be in ascending order.
- The children can now use resource page 126 to make a block graph of their data. Does this help them to draw conclusions from the data? (They should look for simple evidence of correlation – for example, the child with the longest legs jumping the highest.)
- To test things that involve timing (for example, who runs the fastest), a simple 'stopwatch' can be made from a clock with a loud tick. A child counts the number of ticks of the clock while another child runs across the playground.

Differentiation
More able: The children can find the difference between the largest and smallest values measured (for example, the fastest and slowest running time).
Less able: Help the children to decide what to measure and what headings to use for their table on page 81. They may also need help with taking measurements.

Links to other topics
Citizenship: Valuing the differences between people – physical, psychological and cultural.
Literacy: Simple shape poems: tall, short, thin, fat. Stories from Aesop's Fables.

SEE THE PATTERN

Making patterns

■ Write the first letter of your name over and over to make a line on each of the scarves below.

■ Keep the line of letters neat, with the letters touching and all the same.

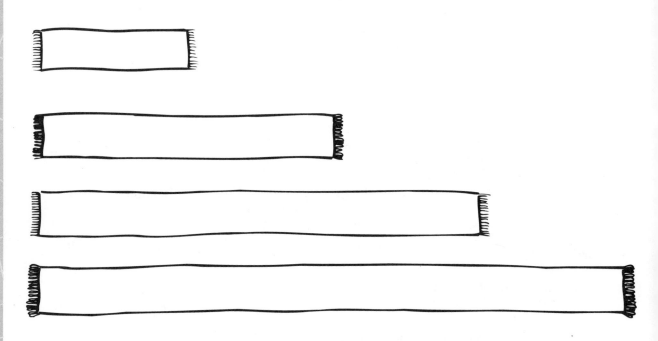

■ Count the number of letters on each scarf.

■ Write the number of letters next to each scarf.

■ Describe the pattern you see.

 Use blocks or beads to make patterns of your own. Draw and describe them on the back of this sheet.

Find the pattern

▓ Look at these containers.

What is the pattern in the size of the containers? _____

_____

▓ Use real containers like the ones shown above. Find out how many beads or blocks fit in each container.
▓ Write the number next to each container shown above.

Can you see a pattern in the number of beads or blocks?
▓ Describe the pattern.

_____

_____

▓ Use beads or blocks to make some more patterns. Can you make patterns with doubles or halves?
▓ Draw and describe them.

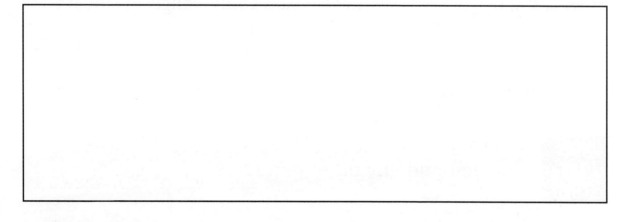

SEE THE PATTERN

Big and little teddies

■ Find out which teddy is the shortest. Write **1** on his tummy.

■ Number the other teddies in order of height.

■ Complete this sentence:

I predict that the teddy with the longest arms is number _____

■ Measure them.
Was your prediction correct? _____

How is the height of the teddies linked to the length of their arms?

_____

_____

NOW TRY THIS   Can you find any other patterns?

Is there a pattern?

◾ Write down your class prediction.

What will you measure?

◾ Fill in this table. Use your own headings. An example has been provided for you.

What we looked at (How long our legs are)	What we measured (How far we can jump)
(Fiona – 70cm)	(Fiona – jumped 1m 20cm)

◾ Write your table out again on another copy of this page. This time, put the people in order with the smallest number first.

Do you think your prediction was correct?
◾ Explain why.

MOVING ON

MATHS FOCUS: RECOGNISING PATTERNS AND RELATIONSHIPS

Learning objectives
- To recognise simple patterns or relationships, generalise and predict.
- To solve simple word problems involving numbers and measures.
- To use number sentences to explain how a problem was solved.

Resources
- Ways of measuring length in uniform non-standard units (such as straws and complete ruler lengths), Blu-Tack, a slinky toy.
- Photocopiable pages 84 (page 85 for less able children) and 86 for each child.

Introduction
5 mins
- Show the children a classroom object (such as a display board) and ask: *How can we find out how long this is?* Discuss ways of measuring it. Demonstrate how to measure the object using a range of uniform non-standard units, such as hand spans and straw lengths.

Whole-class, teacher-directed activity
15 mins
- Show the children two objects that they cannot move to place side by side, such as a desk and a cupboard. Ask: *Which is longer?* Measure them both, using uniform non-standard units (such as straw lengths). *How much longer is the cupboard?* Use Blu-tack to fasten straws to the shorter object. Fasten the same number of straws to the longer object. Count how many more need to be added to make the cupboard's length. Show the children how to write this as a number sentence:

  [desk's length] + [extra straws] = [cupboard's length]
  The cupboard is _____ straws longer than the desk.

- Ask: *How many desks could we fit across the room?* Measure one desk in straw lengths. Measure the distance across the room in straw lengths. Write the relationship as a number sentence: if the desk is 4 straws long, write *4 + 4...* and so on to equal the total distance across the room. (Measure the latter beforehand, so that you can surreptitiously adjust the measurement of the desk or the room to get an exact number of desks.)

Children's activity
20 mins
- Show the children the Slinky. Demonstrate how it can tumble down steps or over the edge of an object. Ask the children to work individually, using cubes, number lines or other apparatus to solve the problem on photocopiable page 84. (The Slinky moves one step at a time; in this problem, it can get down three steps each time it is pushed).

SCIENCE LINK ACTIVITY

Photocopiable page 86 presents an addition problem in the context of looking at how far toy cars travel. The children are given the distance that a toy car travels when pushed by each of two different children. They have to work out which child would have to push the car to make it travel certain distances.

Differentiation
More able: The children can work in pairs to find the answer to a question such as: *How much taller is the desk than the chair?* and write a number sentence.
Less able: The children can use photocopiable page 85. This presents a similar problem to that on page 84, but requires the children to count in twos.

Plenary
10 mins
Ask children to set you problems of the type: *How much longer...* or *How many will fit...?* Ask other children to give you instructions on how to solve each problem.

SCIENCE FOCUS: FORCES AND MOVEMENT (QCA UNIT 2E)

Learning objectives

- To suggest a question to test, then predict what will happen.
- To decide what to do, take measurements and record them in a table.
- To evaluate whether a test was fair.
- To say whether the prediction was correct.

Resources

- A board or flip chart and marker pens, boards and blocks to make ramps of varying heights, metre rulers (or a method of measuring using uniform non-standard units such as straws), toy cars.
- A copy of photocopiable page 87 for each child.

Introduction
5 mins

- Set up a sloping ramp where all the children can see it. Show them a toy car and ask them to suggest ways of making it move. Some children may be familiar with toy car tracks that start with a slope. When they have suggested using the slope, ask them to explain what the slope is for – 'To make the car go fast' or 'To make the car go a long way'.

Whole-class, teacher-directed activity
10 mins

- Let the toy car roll down the ramp and off the end. Ask the children to suggest ways of measuring how far it rolls. Stress the importance of marking the start and finish points in order to measure accurately.
- Ask: *What things could we change to make the car roll a different distance?* Write the children's ideas on the board. Focus on two ideas: how high the ramp goes and how far up the ramp the car is released from. Help the children form one of these ideas into a question that can be tested, such as: *Does making the ramp higher change how far the car rolls?*
- Discuss ways of testing the children's questions. *What will you have to change? What will you have to measure?* Show them how they can use the table on photocopiable page 87 to record their results (they should note the unit of length they used in the table headings). Talk about ways of making the test a fair one – for example: *It wouldn't be fair if sometimes you just let the car go and sometimes you pushed it.*

Children's activity
20–25 mins

- Working in groups, the children can investigate one of two questions – either: *Does changing the height of the ramp change how far the car goes?* or *Does changing how far up the ramp the car starts change how far it goes?* The group should decide what measurements to take and decide on simple ways to make the test fair – for example: 'We will always measure to where the back of the car stops.'
- Encourage the children to discuss how they can use their results to reach a conclusion. (For example, if the car travelled the furthest from the highest ramp, that could be taken to prove that the higher the ramp, the further the car travels.) Ask each group to make up one sentence to explain to the rest of the class what they have found out.

Differentiation

More able: Can the children predict how far the car will go with the next height of the ramp, or the next distance up the ramp? Ask them to predict and then to test their prediction.
Less able: Tell the children which question to investigate (changing the height of the ramp is easier, with the car always starting at the top). Help them to fill in the results table on page 87.

Links to other topics

Geography: Why rivers always go downhill – they 'run down the slope'.
Transport: Why airports have long runways and motorways have long sliproads.

CALCULATIONS AND SOLVING PROBLEMS
PHOTOCOPIABLE

MOVING ON

Down the steps

This Slinky can roll down **3** steps each time it is pushed.

How many pushes will it need to reach the bottom? _____

■ Write a number sentence to show the answer.

This Slinky can roll down 4
steps each time it is pushed.
Find out how many pushes it
will need to reach the bottom.
Write a number sentence.

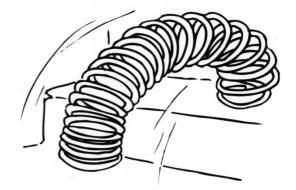

Down the steps

This Slinky can roll down 2 steps each time it is pushed.

How many pushes will it need to reach the bottom? _____

■ Write a number sentence to show the answer.

How many steps would the Slinky go down if you gave it 4 pushes?

■ Write a number sentence to show the answer.

Pushing toy cars

Lucy and Ben push the same toy car.
🔲 Look how far it goes.

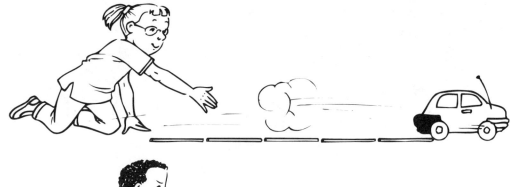

When Lucy and Ben both push the car,
it goes a total distance of 9 straw lengths.

The number sentence to show this is: 5 + 4 = 9

Who should push the car next to make
the total distance 13 straw lengths?   _____

🔲 Write the number sentence.

_____

Who should push the car instead, after
it has gone 9 straw lengths, to make
the total distance 14 straw lengths?   _____

🔲 Write the number sentence.

_____

How far does a toy car go?

■ Do Activity 1 **or** Activity 2.

Activity 1: Changing the height of the ramp

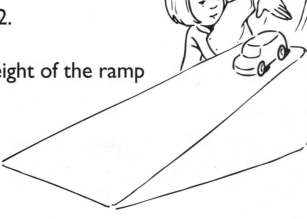

■ Fill in this table.

Height of ramp	Distance the car went

Activity 2: Changing how far up the car starts

■ Fill in this table.

Distance up ramp	Distance the car went

NOW TRY THIS Whether you did Activity 1 or Activity 2, explain to your teacher how you made your test fair.

MEASURES

HOW DO THEY GROW?

MATHS FOCUS: USING THE LANGUAGE OF COMPARISON

Learning objective
■ To understand and use appropriate language to compare number, length and size.

Resources
■ A small piece of play dough (or similar) for each child; a small board for each child (optional).
■ Photocopiable pages 90 (page 91 for less able children) and 92 for each child.

Introduction
5 mins
■ Have a 'question and answer' session to establish the children's understanding of words such as *taller/shorter, longer/shorter, wider/narrower, more/fewer*. Use challenges such as:
  ▪ *Ben, stand here. Emily, can you make yourself taller/shorter than Ben?*
  ▪ *Ashley, hold up some fingers – you choose how many. Craig, can you hold up more/fewer fingers than Ashley?*
  ▪ *Amelia, can you make the gap between these two chairs wider/narrower?*

Whole-class, teacher-directed activity
10 mins
■ The children will need to sit at their desks for this activity, or you will need to provide them with a small board each to work on.
■ Give each child a small amount of play dough. Tell the children: *I am going to make some models, and I want you to copy what I make. But I want you to change your shape so it is different from mine. I will tell you how.*
■ Make a simple snake or worm from play dough. Instruct the children: *Make your snake longer/shorter than mine.*
■ Repeat with other play dough models and other comparing words. (For example: *Make your snowman wider than mine. Make your tree shorter than mine.*) Extend this by asking pairs of children to compare their models with each other. *Compare your tree with the person next to you. Put up your hand if your tree is taller.* Check that their responses are correct.

Children's activity
20 mins
■ The children can use page 90 to compare drawings of objects, identifying the correct comparison words for them and making their own drawings to match further comparisons.

Differentiation
More able: The children can work in pairs to make up and draw their own sets of objects, labelling them with appropriate comparison words. They should include words such as *longest*, *shortest* and *widest*. Check that they understand the difference between 'longer' (comparison of two objects) and 'longest' (comparison of three or more objects).

Less able: The children can complete photocopiable page 91. This sheet involves makes comparisons between two given objects only, matching the correct labels to the objects.

SCIENCE LINK ACTIVITY

Photocopiable page 92 shows a large diagram of a plant, with stems that vary in size and number of leaves. From the set of labels provided, the children need to identify labels that are opposites (for example, *longer* and *shorter*) and then find the appropriate places on the plant to put these labels. One completed pair of labels is provided on the diagram.

Plenary
10 mins
■ Ask the children to describe how they knew, or found out, which of two objects was the taller, wider and so on. They could probably 'just tell by looking'. Discuss how we can compare objects that are very similar, or objects that are a large distance apart. Direct, side-by-side comparison can be used for objects that are similar. Some type of measurement, using standard or uniform non-standard units, is necessary to compare objects that are far apart.

MATHS SKILLS FOR SCIENCE: YEARS 1&2

SCIENCE FOCUS: LIVING THINGS IN THE LOCAL ENVIRONMENT (QCA UNIT 2B)

Learning objectives
- To observe the growth of seedlings and make a day-by-day record of observations.
- To draw conclusions about the conditions that seedlings need to grow.
- To decide whether their conclusions agree with their original expectations.

Resources
- A board or flip chart and marker pens, a large packet of fast-growing seeds, such as mustard, broad beans or sunflowers.
- Small transparent containers, kitchen towels, potting compost, sticky labels.
- A copy of photocopiable page 93 for each child.

Introduction
10 mins
- Show the children the seeds. Ask: *What do you think these seeds need to make them grow?* Record all the children's ideas on the board. Guide them towards two ideas: *water* and *soil*.

Whole-class, teacher-directed activity
10 mins
- Choose the two ideas *water* and *soil*, and put them into the form of questions that the children can investigate. Suitable questions might be: *Do seeds need water to grow?* and *Do seeds need soil to grow?* Ask the children to predict the answers to these questions. Record their predictions on the board.
- The children do not, at this stage, need to know that seeds need warmth, and they will prefer to see quick results, so a comparison of seeds in cold and in warmth is not advisable. Comparison of growth in light and dark conditions is also best avoided. Seedlings grown in the dark grow taller (but thinner and paler) than those grown in the light. At this stage, this may mislead the children into thinking that plants grow better in the dark.
- Discuss with the children how the questions can be investigated. Show them how to set up containers of seeds to investigate each question – for example, a container with seeds on damp soil and a container with seeds on dry soil; or a container with seeds on damp soil and a container with seeds on damp kitchen paper.
- Put the children into small groups and make sure that each group knows which question they will investigate. Make sure that approximately half the class investigate each question.

Children's activity
20–25 mins
- Working in small groups, the children should set up two containers of seeds (one dry and one wet, or one with soil and one with paper). They should label their containers, then keep a day-by-day record of their observations of the growth of the seeds. They can use photocopiable page 93 to record their results, by writing or by drawing.
- Use class discussion to help establish what the children have found out about the conditions that seeds need to grow. They should have found that the seeds need water, but do not need soil. Is this what they predicted?

Differentiation
More able: Ask the children to compare the ways in which different seedlings grow, rather than just the length of the seedling. Are they all the same? They should find the growth patterns similar in some ways (the seedlings all grow roots before leaves) and different in other ways (they do not all grow the same number of leaves or grow leaves of the same size).
Less able: Help the children to plan an investigation into the effects of wet and dry conditions on seed growth. Help them to generalise from the class results: *All seeds need water to grow.*

Links to other topics
Geography: Some countries have desert regions where not many plants can grow, because there is not much water.
Music/Drama: Modelling the growth of roots and shoots from seeds.

HOW DO THEY GROW?

What size is it?

▧ Draw a line to match the right label to each picture.

| shorter | taller | even shorter |

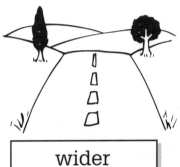 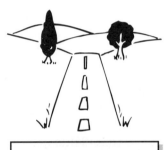 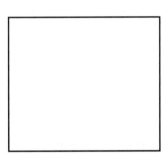

| wider | narrower | even narrower |

  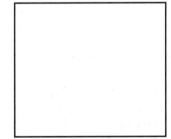

| fewer | more | even more |

▧ Draw one more picture in each row.

| more | least | fewer | shorter | taller |
| tallest | wider | narrower | widest |

 On another sheet of paper, draw more sets of
pictures. Use the labels in the box above.

MATHS SKILLS FOR SCIENCE: YEARS 1&2

How big?

Match these words to the right pictures.

taller

shorter

wider

narrower

more

fewer

MEASURES

PHOTOCOPIABLE

Match the labels

▨ Look at this list of words. Can you find pairs of words that are opposites?

thicker	more	thinner	longer
lower	shorter	fewer	higher

▨ Write the words around this plant in the right places.

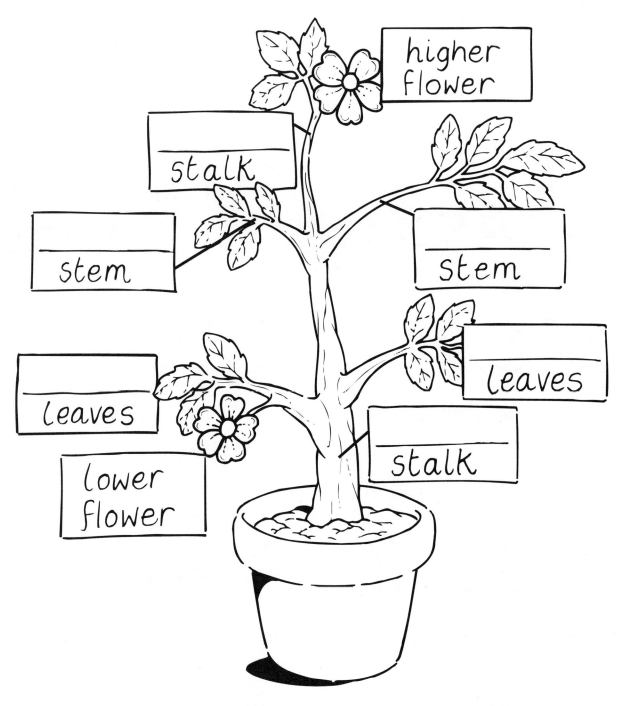

What do seeds need to grow?

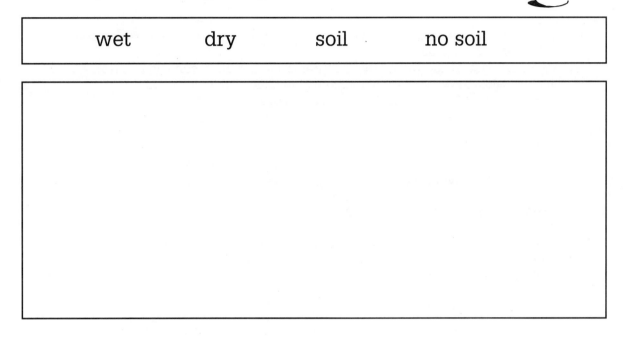

▨ Draw how you planted your seeds in the box below.
▨ Label your drawing, using words from this list:

wet	dry	soil	no soil

What did you see happening to the seeds each day?
▨ Write or draw what happened in this table.

Day 1	
Day 2	
Day 3	
Day 4	

▨ Continue the table on the back of this sheet.

CHANGING FOOD

MATHS FOCUS: USING MEASURING APPARATUS

Learning objectives
■ To use standard or non-standard units to measure mass.
■ To choose appropriate simple measuring apparatus.
■ To use simple fractions for estimation.

Resources
■ A range of different measuring scales or balances and different-sized measuring spoons; rice, flour, pasta, dried peas.
■ Ingredients for making shortbread (flour, butter or margarine, caster sugar), clean kitchen equipment (scales, tablespoons, a blunt knife, round aluminium foil trays).
■ Photocopiable pages 96, 97 (page 98 for less able children) for each child.

Introduction
Up to 5 mins
■ Discuss with the children when we need to weigh things: cooking and preparing food, buying vegetables, buying sweets, weighing ourselves and so on.

Whole-class, teacher-directed activity
10–15 mins
■ Show the children a range of measuring apparatus, such as balance scales, scales with simple dials, digital scales and spoons of different sizes.
■ Demonstrate how to use these, and allow the children to practise. *Weigh out 100g of rice on this set of scales – where should the needle point to on the dial? How much does one tablespoonful of flour weigh?* and so on.

Children's activity
20–25 mins
■ The children can practise using a range of different measuring apparatus, working to complete photocopiable page 96. They may need help in deciding when they should approximate – for example, 'approximately 4 tablespoons of dried peas weigh 100g'.

Differentiation (see 'Science link activity')
More able: Ask the children whether they can recognise a pattern in the amounts of flour, butter and sugar used. (It is a simple 3 : 2 : 1 pattern.) Can they use this pattern to work out how much of the other ingredients they will need if they start with 300g of flour? Can they work out how much of each ingredient they would need to make 16 pieces instead of 8?
Less able: The children can follow the shortbread recipe on photocopiable page 98, which involves using non-standard units. Provide a 200g block of butter or margarine: the children will need to find ¼ of this. Encourage careful measurement, and ask the children why it is important to have the right amounts of all the different ingredients in the recipe.

SCIENCE LINK ACTIVITY

Photocopiable pages 97 and 98 show a simple recipe for making shortbread. Page 97 uses standard units, page 98 uses non-standard units. Use page 97 with most children. If these sheets are laminated, the children can use the recipes while they are cooking. The recipe requires the children to measure out ingredients, then mark the shortbread into eight equal pieces before cooking. They can do this by halving the circle repeatedly.

Plenary
10 mins
■ Recap on how to use the different types of measuring apparatus, asking individual children to demonstrate and explain how they used the apparatus to weigh out certain quantities and to find the weights of certain volumes (for example, a cup of rice).
■ Show the children the recipe on page 98. Explain why these non-standard measures are useful: we can use them to make the shortbread at home, even if we do not have any kitchen scales there.

SCIENCE FOCUS: GROUPING AND CHANGING MATERIALS (QCA UNIT 2D)

Learning objectives
- To observe and explore the ways in which materials change.
- To know that materials often change when they are heated.
- **Extra activity:** To know that some materials change when they are cooled.

Resources
- Pictures or samples of bread and toast, raw and cooked egg.
- For teacher use only: a raw egg, a saucepan half-full of boiling water, a small metal container that will float.
- A range of familiar materials: sugar, salt, butter or margarine, chocolate, golden syrup, ice cubes or ice cream.
- Bowls of hot water (hand-hot from tap only) and ice, small metal containers (small pie or tart cases), teaspoons, small beakers of warm water.
- A copy of photocopiable page 99 for each child.

Introduction
5 mins
- Show the children the pictures or samples of bread and egg before and after cooking. Ask: *What has happened to the bread and the egg? What happened to make them change?* Discuss other things that change when heated. Can the children think of other ways of making things change apart from heating them? (Probably not at this stage.)

Whole-class, teacher-directed activity
10 mins
- Crack a raw egg into a small metal container. Ask the children to describe it. Ask them to predict what will happen if you put the container of egg on a bowl of boiling water. Try this. (**SAFETY:** keep the hot water well out of the children's reach.) After a few minutes, the egg will show signs of cooking around the edge.
- Ask: *How else could we make things change?* Prompt the children to think of cooling instead of heating, and of mixing things together (for example, mixing powders with water).
- Demonstrate the effect of mixing sugar or salt with water. Ask the children to describe the materials before and after mixing. Some children may already know the word 'dissolve'.

Children's activity
20–25 mins
- Ask the children to explore different ways of making materials change, using photocopiable page 99 to guide their planning and recording. They can try heating the material (by putting it above a bowl of hot water) or mixing it with water (by stirring it into a beaker of water). The children in each group should choose one thing to try – for example, 'finding the effect of heating all the different materials' or 'finding different ways of making sugar change'.
- **Extra activity:** Children who finish the activity early could be encouraged to try the effect of cooling the material (by putting it above a bowl of ice).

Differentiation
More able: Ask the children to predict the result before investigating, then test their prediction. Ask them to think of an everyday example of how a change they have looked at is used.
Less able: Help the children to decide what to investigate (for example, the effect of heating different materials). Help them to focus on the type of change they might look for (for example, the material going runnier or changing colour), and how they will record their results.

Links to other topics
Ourselves: Cooking and food hygiene – why we must wash our hands before handling food, and only use clean apparatus.
Art: How materials such as clay and salt dough change when they are heated, or when they dry out. Making models with these materials. Making models or collages with dried plant material (flowers, leaves, seeds). Discussing why dried materials are useful.
Literacy: Writing instructions for cooking food (recipes) or for carrying out investigations.

Measuring apparatus

▓ Label these pieces of measuring apparatus.
One has been done for you.

teacup

▓ Find out how much these amounts weigh. Don't weigh the container, only what it contains.

I cup of rice _____

2 cups of pasta _____

I teaspoon of flour _____

I tablespoon of flour _____

▓ Find the answers to these questions. Use just one type of measure each time. Your answer may be approximate.

What volume of dried peas weighs 100g? _____

What volume of flour weighs 50g? _____

What volume of rice weighs 30g? _____

Making shortbread

You will need:

Ingredients
- 75g flour
- 50g butter or margarine
- 25g sugar

What to do

■ Mix all the ingredients to a smooth paste.

■ Put the mixture into a round tin and press it down.

■ Mark the mixture into 8 pieces.

■ Ask an adult to cook the shortbread for 20 minutes in a cool oven (160°C or Gas Mark 3).

NOW TRY THIS How much of each ingredient would you need to make 16 shortbread pieces the same size as before?

Making shortbread

You will need:

flour

tablespoon

mixing bowl

sugar

butter or margarine

round aluminium foil tray

knife

> ### Ingredients
> - 1 rounded tablespoon flour
> - ¼ block butter or margarine
> - 1 level tablespoon sugar

What to do

Mix all the ingredients to a smooth paste.

Put the mixture into a round tin and press it down.

Mark the mixture into **8** pieces.

Ask an adult to cook the shortbread for **20** minutes in a cool oven (160°C or Gas Mark 3).

Making things change

Here are some ways of making materials change.

Heating

Cooling

Mixing with water

What are you going to investigate?

■ Record your results. Use writing or drawing.

NOW TRY THIS

Describe one everyday situation where a material changes.

SHAPE AND SPACE

3-D SHAPES

MATHS FOCUS: DESCRIBING 3-D SHAPES

Learning objectives
- To know the names of common 3-D shapes.
- To describe some features of 3-D shapes.
- To sort 3-D shapes according to their properties.

Resources
- A selection of 2-D and 3-D shapes with card labels stating their names.
- A set of 'description cards' from photocopiable page 104.
- A selection of everyday objects with recognisable 3-D shapes (cans, boxes, balls and so on).
- A copy of photocopiable page 102 (page 103 for less able children) for each child.

Preparation: Use photocopiable page 104 to make a set of 'description cards'.

Introduction
Up to 5 mins
- Show the children some 2-D shapes. *Who can tell me what this shape is called?* Help them to describe the different shapes. *How many sides has this got? Are the sides straight or curved? Are the sides all the same length?*

Whole-class, teacher-directed activity
10 mins
- Display some 3-D shapes with card name labels. Help the children to describe them. *How many faces has this got? Are the faces flat or curved? What shapes are the flat faces?*
- Describe a 3-D shape and ask for a volunteer to find the shape matching your description. Ask the other children whether the volunteer found the right shape.
- Take away the name labels. Help the children to find the correct labels for the shapes, and then to find the correct shapes for the labels.
- Ask the children to name and describe the shapes of some familiar objects. For example, 'A can is a cylinder. Two of its faces are circles. The third face is a rectangle rolled up.'

Children's activity
20–25 mins
- The children can work individually to complete photocopiable page 102, an activity sheet on recognising and describing common 3-D shapes.
- Then they can play 'Guess the shape' in pairs. Give each pair some shapes, including familiar objects. One child chooses a shape, holds it out of sight and describes a feature of it (for example, 'It has straight edges'). He or she describes the shape's features one at a time until the second child can try to guess the shape. If the guess is correct, the second child selects a shape. If it is wrong, the first child chooses another shape.

SCIENCE LINK ACTIVITY

This can be a teacher-led or group activity. Give each child one or more 'description cards' from page 104. The teacher or group leader holds up an everyday object (such as a cardboard cylinder). The children hold up any cards they have that match this object's properties (such as *circular face, curved face, dull, bendy*). The children decide whether the cards held up are correct, and whether any other describing words could be added.

Differentiation
More able: The children can use a more difficult selection of shapes, including pyramids and/or triangular prisms. Challenge them to describe their shape without touching it or looking at it.

Less able: The children can use photocopiable page 103. They can play 'Guess the shape' with just cubes, cylinders and spheres.

Plenary
10 mins
- Recap briefly on some features of 3-D shapes. *What is this shape called? Tell me one feature of it.*
- Play '10 questions', with the children trying to identify a shape you have chosen. You can only answer *Yes* or *No* to their questions. (They are not allowed to ask questions such as 'Is it a cube?')

3-D SHAPES

SCIENCE FOCUS: GROUPING AND CHANGING MATERIALS (QCA UNIT 2D)

Learning objectives
- To know that different materials have a range of different properties.
- To explore different materials, making observations and simple comparisons.
- To explore melting ice using appropriate senses.

Resources
- Some ornaments made from wood, metal, glass and rock.
- Pictures of ice sculptures and people making them.
- Ice shapes (large shapes last longer, but a few small shapes for each group might be preferable), large shallow trays.
- Different modelling materials (clay, Plasticine, salt dough and Blu-Tack).
- A copy of photocopiable page 105 for each child.

Preparation: Most common 3-D shapes are easy to make from ice. You can make cubes and cuboids by freezing water-filled boxes; pyramids by tilting a box so that only one corner is filled with water; cones by lining a funnel with aluminium foil, filling it with water and freezing it upright; and spheres by freezing water-filled balloons, then removing the balloon.

Introduction
5 mins
- Ask: *What different shapes do you know?* Make sure the children can distinguish between 2-D shapes and 3-D shapes. Discuss the features of some common 3-D shapes.

Whole-class, teacher-directed activity
10 mins
- Show the children some ornaments made from different materials. *All these ornaments have been made from different materials. Do you know what the materials are? How easy do you think it is to make the ornaments?* Discuss the properties of the different materials that make them easy or hard to shape. Ask the children what materials would it be easy to make different shapes from (clay, salt dough and so on). Discuss the properties that make these materials easy to shape.
- Show the children some pictures of ice sculptures. Discuss how these are made, and how easy it is to shape water before freezing it. *How does water change when it turns to ice? How can we make ice? What do you think will happen to these ice sculptures? Why?*

Children's activity
20–25 mins
- Ask the children to work in groups, making some familiar 3-D shapes (cube, cuboid, sphere, cylinder) from a range of different modelling materials. They can use photocopiable page 105 to help them consider the differences between the materials.
- Ask each group to describe some of the 3-D ice shapes you have provided, and to observe how they change with time (as they melt).

Differentiation
More able: Ask the children to suggest ways to stop ice shapes or ice sculptures from melting, or to make them melt more slowly.
Less able: Give the children some examples of simple 3-D shapes, with labels, to copy in their modelling.

Links to other topics
Geography: Weather – how ice and snow affect us and the landscape. How snow melts, and what happens to the water. Children around the world living or going to school where it is snowy.
Citizenship: People who help us – caretakers at school, who have to clear up the mess left from modelling! The importance of helping them by keeping the classroom clean and tidy.

3-D shapes

■ Name these shapes.

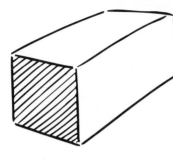
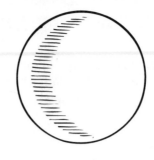
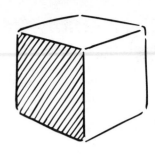

_____ _____

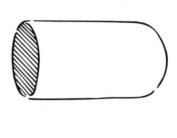
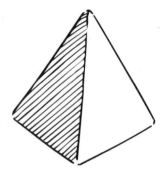

_____

_____

■ Name **one** shape with

_____

a curved face _____

a flat face _____

Which shape matches
the description below? _____

It has straight edges.
It has six faces.
All the faces are squares.

Choose a 3-D shape. Write your own description of it.

_____

_____

3-D shapes

■ Draw a line to match each shape to its name.

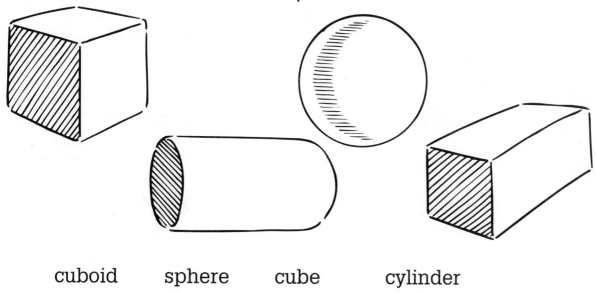

cuboid   sphere   cube   cylinder

■ Match these shapes to their descriptions.

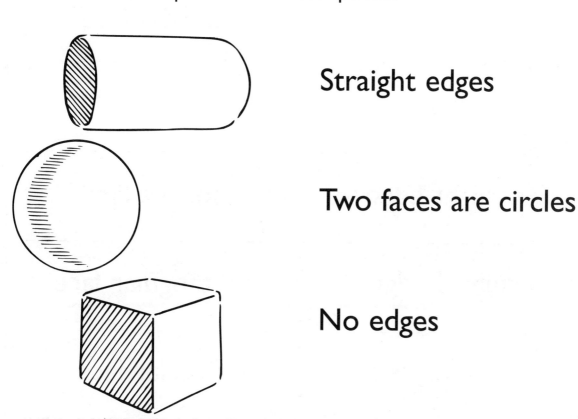

Straight edges

Two faces are circles

No edges

■ Write another feature of a cube.

3-D SHAPES

Description cards

hard	4 edges
soft	5 edges
bendy	2 edges
stiff	flat face
shiny	curved face
dull	flat and curved faces
straight edge	square face
curved edge	rectangular face
no edges	circular face
6 edges	triangular face

3-D SHAPES

Modelling materials

▨ Use some different modelling materials to make these shapes.

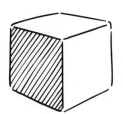 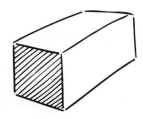  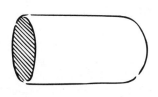

Which material was the easiest to use?

_____

What properties made it easy to use?

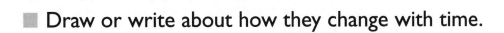

▨ Draw your ice shapes. Name them.

▨ Draw or write about how they change with time.

NOW TRY THIS   How could you stop the ice shapes changing?

MATHS FOCUS: PRESENTING INFORMATION IN A TABLE

Learning objectives
- To collect data and make a simple table.
- To respond to questions about the data in a table.

Resources
- A small piece of card (approximately one-eighth of A4 size) for each child, felt-tip pens, a board or flip chart, marker pens.
- Photocopiable pages 108 (page 109 for less able children) and 110 for each child.

Preparation: Make sure that a selection of tables are on display around the classroom: the names of children in different groups, odd and even numbers, simple timetables showing activities on different days, and so on.

Introduction
Up to 5 mins
- Show the children one of the tables on display. Talk about what it tells them. Explain that tables give us information in a simple form. Ask: *Can anyone see any more tables in the classroom?* Ask the children what information the other tables are giving them.

Whole-class, teacher-directed activity
10 mins
- Tell the children: *We are going to make a table to show how many brothers and sisters the children in this class have.* Pass round the pieces of card and pens. Ask the children to write on the card the number of brothers and sisters they have, using large numerals that can be read from a distance.
- On the board or flip chart, write the heading 'Our brothers and sisters'. Draw a 5-column table with the headings '0' to '4'. Ask the children with no brothers or sisters to hold up their cards. Write their names in the column headed '0'. Repeat with other numbers of brothers and sisters.
- Ask questions such as:
  - *How many children have two brothers or sisters?*
  - *Name someone with one brother or sister.*
  Help the children to use the table to find the answers.
- The children should keep their cards for the next part of the lesson.

Children's activity
20–25 mins
- Ask each child to write his or her name, and the names of all his or her brothers and sisters, on the back of the card. Working in groups, the children can use photocopiable page 108 to make a table showing the names with 3, 4, 5, 6 and more than 6 letters. They should include the names of all the children in the group and all their brothers and sisters.

SCIENCE LINK ACTIVITY

Photocopiable page 108 shows a picture of a kitchen with fridge magnets attached to some objects, and lines to show where they have fallen from other objects. The children can use the information in the picture to make a table showing what things the magnets stuck to and what things they didn't.

Differentiation
More able: The children can use the table on page 108 to find out how many children there are altogether in the group's families. They can check this by counting the names written on the cards.
Less able: The children can use page 109 to make a table of the names of all the children in the group.

Plenary
10 mins
- Draw a copy of the table from photocopiable page 108. Write the name of a character from a familiar story. Can the children put the name in the correct column? Ask: *How many names have 3 letters?* Encourage the children to make up and answer similar questions.

SCIENCE FOCUS: MAGNETISM (BUILDING ON QCA UNIT 1C)

Learning objectives
- To explore the effects of magnets.
- To classify materials as magnetic or non-magnetic.
- To compare the strength of different magnets.

This unit relates to the Scottish 5–14 Guidelines: Forces and their effects, Level C.

Resources
- A selection of different magnets (including fridge magnets), paper clips.
- A selection of small objects, some made from magnetic materials and some from non-magnetic materials.
- A copy of photocopiable page 111 for each child.

Introduction
Up to 5 mins
- Ask the children to talk about where they have seen magnets. Most children will have seen fridge magnets. They may have used magnetic letters and boards, either at home or school. Most of them will not know that a magnetic board is metal – do not tell them at this stage.

Whole-class, teacher-directed activity
10 mins
- Show the children a selection of magnets, including some fridge magnets. Can they identify the part of a fridge magnet that is really a magnet?
- Ask: *Do all materials stick to magnets?* Ask the children how they could find out which objects stick to magnets and which don't. Ask them to suggest ways of recording the results. If necessary, remind them of their work on making tables.
- If the children are already familiar with magnets from work done in QCA Unit 1C, discuss whether all magnets are as strong as each other. Ask the children how they could compare how strong different magnets are. Discuss their ideas, including how they would collect and record the results.
- Explain to the children that magnets can damage some things. Stress that they must not hold magnets near computers, videotapes or cassette tapes, because these electronic items will be damaged if they do. Remind them that they must not put fridge magnets near these things at home either.

Children's activity
20–25 mins
- The children can explore a selection of objects made from a range of different materials to find out which stick to a magnet and which don't. Allow them to explore different objects around the classroom as well. Encourage them to compare the strength of two or three different magnets, and provide paper clips for them to use for this. They can use photocopiable page 111 to record their results.
- Challenge the children to solve problems involving magnets. Can they explain why magnetic letters and numbers stick to a special board? Sometimes cupboard doors have magnets in them, and the cupboard has small metal plates. Can the children explain what these are for?

Differentiation
More able: Challenge the children to write a few sentences describing how they compared the strength of different magnets. Can they explain what they found out? For example: 'We knew this magnet was stronger because it pulled harder' or '...because it pulled more paper clips' or '...because paper clips jumped onto it from further away.'
Less able: Challenge the children to find three objects that stick to a magnet and three objects that don't.

Links to other topics
Art: Use stiff card and small magnets to make fridge magnets. Make a magnetic fishing game, magnetic boats game or magnetic racing game.
Literacy: Write instructions for how to play a magnetic game.

MAKING A TABLE

How many letters?

Your cards show the names of all the children in your families.

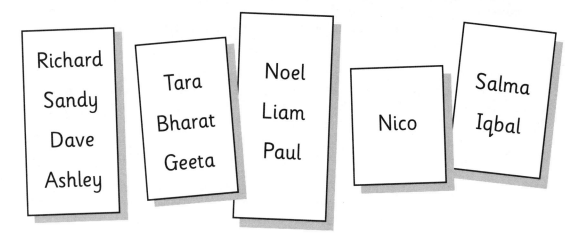

Richard
Sandy
Dave
Ashley

Tara
Bharat
Geeta

Noel
Liam
Paul

Nico

Salma
Iqbal

How many letters are there in each name on your group's cards?
Make a table.

Names in our families

3 letters	4 letters	5 letters	6 letters	More than 6 letters

How many of the names have 4 letters? _____

Write a name with 5 letters in the table.
How many letters do the biggest group of names have? _____

NOW TRY THIS Use the table to work out how many children there are altogether in your group's families.

How many letters?

How many letters are in your name? _____

▓ Write your name in the correct column of this table.

Letters in our names

3 letters	4 letters	5 letters	6 letters	More than 6 letters

▓ Write all your group's names in the table.

How many of the names have 4 letters? _____

▓ Write another name in the table with the same number of letters as your name.

▓ Count how many names there are in the table altogether.

MAKING A TABLE

What do fridge magnets stick to?

Some children tried sticking fridge magnets to different things in the kitchen.
Some of the fridge magnets stuck, but some didn't.

■ Make a table to show what the magnets did and didn't stick to.

Things the magnet did stick to	Things the magnet didn't stick to

RECORDING AND ORGANISING DATA
PHOTOCOPIABLE

Finding magnetic things

▓ Use a magnet to explore your classroom. What things will stick to it?
Remember: don't put a magnet near the computer.

▓ Write four things in each of these lists.

Things the magnet did stick to	Things the magnet didn't stick to

▓ Find out how strong two or three different magnets are.

Magnet	What it did

▓ Draw pictures to show what you found out.

MATHS FOCUS: USING A PICTOGRAM

Learning objectives
- To solve a problem by collecting and organising information.
- To present information in a pictogram.

Resources
- Beads, buttons, counters or coloured card circles in four to six colours, Blu-Tack.
- An A3 copy of resource page 125, and two A4 or A3 copies for each group, a copy of photocopiable pages 114 and 115 for each group.

Introduction
5 mins
- Ask several children: *What is your favourite colour?* Then ask the class: *What is the colour that most of you like best? Are you sure? How can we find out?* Discuss the children's ideas for gathering data.

Whole-class, teacher-directed activity
10–15 mins
- Pass round a collection of coloured objects (see 'Resources'). Ask each child to select **one** object in his or her favourite of the available colours.
- Explain to the children that a pictogram is a way of making a picture to show information – in this case, how many children like different colours. Colour the boxes across the bottom of your enlarged copy of page 125 with the same colours as your objects.
- Ask all the children in turn to stick their chosen object to the pictogram in the correct column with Blu-Tack .
- Discuss the most and least popular favourite colours, and how it is possible to know.
- Count the total number of objects on the sheet. Compare that with the number of children in the class.

Children's activity
15–20 mins
- Each group can choose six ice cream flavours and colour in the pictures at the top of a copy of photocopiable page 114, then cut them out and stick them along the bottom of the pictogram sheet to make a pictogram key. Each child can then cut out and colour in **one** ice cream cone picture to show his or her favourite flavour. The children can stick their ice cream pictures on the resource sheet in the correct positions to create a group pictogram.

SCIENCE LINK ACTIVITY

Photocopiable page 115 can be used to make a pictogram showing the types of exercise than the children in Class 2 take. Use this to reinforce the use of pictograms and to give extra practice in drawing them. This activity could also be used, in conjunction with the introductory work for the science lesson, to encourage discussion about why we need exercise.

Differentiation
More able: Ask: *Was there any ice cream flavour that four children liked best?* Ask the children to find the answer and then to make up some similar questions of their own.
Less able: Help the children to decide on three, or even two, ice cream flavours. Provide help with labelling the pictogram and deciding where the individual ice cream pictures should be stuck.

Plenary
10 mins
- Share the group pictograms. Discuss: *Were the favourite ice cream flavours the same for all the groups? Were they the flavours you expected?*

SCIENCE FOCUS: HEALTH AND GROWTH (QCA UNIT 2A)

Learning objectives
- To understand that we need exercise to stay healthy.
- To make and record observations and make simple comparisons.

Resources
- Pictures of children playing various sports, information from local leisure centres about facilities for children, child-safe scissors, adhesive.
- An A3 copy of resource page 125 for each group, a copy of photocopiable pages 116 and 117 for each child.

Introduction
5 mins
- Ask: *What does 'being healthy' mean?* Explain that it means feeling good and being well. Highlight the importance of exercise for staying healthy.

Whole-class, teacher-directed activity
10 mins
- Display some pictures of children playing sports. Can the class name each sport shown?
- Discuss the types of exercise the children do out of school, including 'ordinary' outdoor play activities. Make the children aware of local leisure facilities: swimming, football, dancing and so on.
- Remind the children of the work they have already done on pictograms. Show them an A3 copy of resource page 125. Ask: *What labels does this need to make a pictogram showing what kinds of exercise you do?*

Children's activity
20–25 mins
- The children can work in groups, each group recording the different types of exercise done by the children in the group. They should only include activities they do at least once a week, and limit the total number of activities recorded for the group to six. Each child can use photocopiable page 116 to record the group's results (in writing).
- The group should now be able to make a pictogram sheet recording the types of exercise they do. Each child will need to stick one picture from page 117 onto the group pictogram for each type of exercise he or she does. The children can draw further pictures on page 117 if necessary. They can then use their pictogram to find out which is the most popular type of exercise in their group, and how many of them play football. Do they think a pictogram of adult exercise would look the same?
- If there are single-sex groups, you will be able to discuss any differences between the types of exercise chosen by boys and those chosen by girls.
- For homework, ask the children to collate data from adults at home in order to make another class pictogram. Does it match their prediction on page 116? Why (or why not)?

Differentiation
More able: Ask the children to explain why there are more pictures on the pictogram than children in the group. Ask very able children to find out how many types of exercise each child in the group does. (This could be done, for example, by the children taking turns to cover one square of the pictogram with a counter for every type of exercise they do, and each child remembering how many counters he or she has put on – or by each child using a different coloured counter.)
Less able: Ask the children to decide as a group on between three and five different types of exercise and to make their pictogram using these. Help them with labelling the pictogram.

Links to other topics
PE: Ask keen participants in out-of-school sports to demonstrate, and perhaps teach, some of the skills they have learned to the rest of the class.
Literacy: Ask the children to write to the local leisure centre manager, asking what sports there are for children.

HANDLING AND INTERPRETING DATA

PHOTOCOPIABLE

Favourite ice cream flavours

◼ Choose six different flavours
of ice cream.

◼ Colour them in and label them.

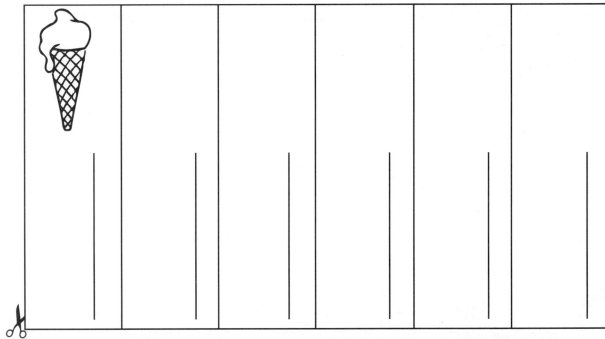

◼ Cut out these ice creams and stick them along the bottom of
your pictogram sheet.

◼ Cut out the ice cream pictures below.

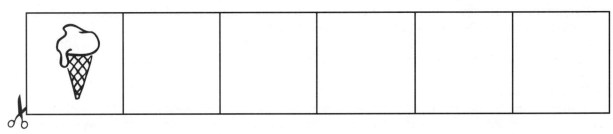

◼ Colour **one** ice cream each to show your favourite flavour.

◼ Stick your ice cream picture in the correct place on your
group pictogram.

Which flavour ice cream
does your group like best? _____

How often do they do exercise?

The children in Class 2 were asked: "How many times each week do you do exercise out of school?" Here are their answers.

■ Cut out the pictures.
■ Use the Pictogram sheet to show how often the children in Class 2 do exercise.

1. How many times each week do the greatest number of children do exercise? _____

2. How many children do no exercise out of school? _____

3. How many children do exercise three or more times each week? _____

 Jack doesn't do any exercise out of school.

NOW TRY THIS   If Jack joins an after-school PE club once each week, how will the pictogram change?

PICTOGRAMS

What kinds of exercise do you do?

What kinds of exercise do your group do?
▢ Make a list.

Type of exercise	Number of children

How many children do each kind of exercise?
▢ Write the numbers in the table above.

▢ Label your pictogram sheet.

▢ Make a pictogram.

Which type of exercise do the
most children in your group do?

_____

How many of you play football? _____

NOW TRY THIS If you asked grown-ups to make a pictogram of the
exercise they do, do you think it would be the same?

Exercise cards

HANDLING AND INTERPRETING DATA

BLOCK GRAPHS

MATHS FOCUS: MAKING A BLOCK GRAPH

Learning objectives
- To collect and organise data.
- To present information as a simple block graph.

Resources
- Coloured pencils, Blu-Tack, a flip chart or board, marker pens, scissors (for less able children).
- For each child: a square of paper (10cm × 10cm).
- An A3 copy of resource page 126 for demonstration; photocopiable pages 120 (page 121 for less able children), 122 and resource page 126 for each child.

Introduction
5 mins
- Ask the children: *How many people live in your house?* Suggest: *I think most children in this class have three people living in their house. Am I right? How do you know?* (They may suggest that teachers are always right!) *How can we find out?*
- Show the children an A3 copy of resource page 126. Explain that they can make a class block graph to find out whether your statement was right.

Whole-class, teacher-directed activity
10–15 mins
- Ask each child to draw all the people who live in his or her house on a paper square. They should include themselves. *Put up your hand if there are four people in your house.* Ask these children to colour their drawings, for example, red. Repeat for different numbers of people and different colours.
- Write the labels *1 person, 2 people* and so on across the bottom of the board. Use Blu-Tack to stick each child's picture above the correct label.
- Ask: *How many houses have three people in? Was what I said about this class right?*
- Ask questions such as: *Why are there no pictures in the '1 person' column? What is the largest/smallest number of people in one house?*
- Discuss how a graph could be made by colouring blocks, rather than sticking on pictures. (Since all the pictures in each column are the same colour, this should be easy for the children to understand.)

Children's activity
20–25 mins
- Ask all the children to write their names in a class table to show how many pets they have. They can work in pairs, using the class table, photocopiable page 120 and resource page 126 to make a block graph showing how many pets the children in this class have. They should colour in the blocks and label the graph, using the labels at the bottom of page 120.

SCIENCE LINK ACTIVITY

Photocopiable page 122 shows a range of electrical appliances in school and at home. The children can use this with a copy of resource page 126 to make a block graph showing how many appliances are used in different places.

Differentiation
More able: The children can work in pairs to write two more questions about the block graph, similar to the question on photocopiable page 120. They can swap questions with another pair and find the answers.

Less able: The children can use photocopiable page 121 and a labelled copy of resource page 126 to make a block graph for the children in their group (limiting the total number to 6 or less).

Plenary
10 mins
- Discuss which numbers of pets were most and least common. *Was the most common number the same for all the groups?* Remind the children that using the same colour for all the squares in one column makes the graph easier to read.

MATHS SKILLS FOR SCIENCE: YEARS 1&2

SCIENCE FOCUS: USING ELECTRICITY (QCA UNIT 2F)

Learning objectives
■ To know that many everyday appliances use electricity.
■ To be aware that electrical appliances include many that heat up, light up, move and produce sound.

Resources
■ Examples of electrical appliances from around the home (hair dryer, torch, battery-powered toy, kettle, electric whisk, electric lamp and so on), colouring pencils.
■ Catalogues or magazines showing pictures of electrical appliances.
■ Photocopiable page 123 and resource page 126 for each child.

Introduction
5 mins
■ Discuss the children's experience of electrical appliances. How many can they name? Where have they seen them or used them?

Whole-class, teacher-directed activity
10–15 mins
■ Show the children some electrical appliances. Point out the lead and plug or where the batteries go. Encourage them to think of more things that use batteries or that are plugged in. Emphasise that these all use electricity.
■ Explain that electricity can come from the mains or from batteries. Discuss electrical safety briefly (though this should form the main focus of at least one lesson). Stress that the children must not plug in any of the appliances they look at in this lesson, nor touch electrical sockets or plugs around the school.
■ Discuss some of the different ways in which electrical appliances could be grouped – for example: *Who uses it? Where is it used? What does it do?*

Children's activity
20–25 mins
■ Ask: *What is electricity used for?* The children can work in groups to find electrical appliances in the classroom or the whole school. They can also find and try to identify different electrical appliances in catalogues or magazines. They should record the appliances they find in the table on photocopiable page 123, grouped according to what the appliances do.
■ They can then use resource page 126 to make individual block graphs showing the number of electrical appliances of each type they found.

Differentiation
More able: Make a statement such as: *Over half the electrical appliances in school make sounds.* Challenge the children to use their graph to find out whether this statement is correct. Ask them to think about the limitations of their data (for example, they are not allowed into the school office or the school kitchen). Do they think the block graph would be the same for a different class or a different school?
Less able: Ask the children to find a maximum of 10 electrical appliances. Help them as necessary to group these appliances. Alternatively, provide 10 to 20 items and ask the children to select the ones that use electricity, then group and record them. They can use two or three simple groups, such as *uses batteries* and *uses mains* or *used at school, used at home* and *used at school and at home.* Give them block graphs with the axes already labelled.

Links to other topics
Literacy: Writing safety notices or instructions on how to use an electrical appliance safely.
PSHE: Considering the dangers of electricity – safe and unsafe things to do and places to play.
Music: Looking at electrical musical instruments (such as keyboards and guitars) and discos.
History: Trying to imagine life before electricity. Looking at lamps, candles, traditional kettles, clockwork toys and so on.

BLOCK GRAPHS

How many pets?

Count how many children in the class have no pets.

Write the number in this table.

How many pets?	Number of children
0	
1	
2	
3	
4	
5	

Do the same for the other numbers of pets in the table.

Make a block graph to show how many pets the children in the class have.

Cut out the labels below.

Put them in the right places on your graph.

What is the most common number
of pets for the children in your class? _____

NOW TRY THIS Can you make up some more questions to answer with your block graph? Write them on the back of this sheet.

✂ -

Number of pets	Number of children

Block graph to show how many pets the children in our class have

How many pets in our group?

▨ Write your name in the correct square.
▨ Do the same for everyone in your group.

I have 0 pets.

I have 1 pet.

I have 2 pets.

I have 3 or more pets.

How many children have no pets?
▨ Colour in that many squares
on your 'Block graph sheet'.

How many children have 1 pet?
▨ Colour in the squares.
▨ Do the same for 2 pets, then for 3 or more pets.
▨ Complete this sentence:

Most children in our group have _____ pets.

BLOCK GRAPHS

Where do we use electricity?

The children in Class 2 looked for things that use electricity.
This is what they found:

School   How many? ☐

Kitchen   How many? ☐

Bedroom   How many? ☐

Living room   How many? ☐

Other   How many? ☐

▪ Use the 'Block graph sheet' to draw a block graph showing how many electrical things there are in each place.

How many electrical things are there in the kitchen? _____

How many electrical things are shown altogether? _____

NOW TRY THIS   How else could you group these electrical things?

BLOCK GRAPHS

What is electricity used for?

▦ Find some things in school and at home that use electricity. Think about what they do.

▦ Record them in this table.

Makes sound	Makes light	Makes warmth	Moves	Something else
How many?	How many?	How many?	How many?	How many?

▦ Make a block graph to show what electricity is used for. Use the 'Block graph sheet' and the labels at the bottom of this page.

John says: "Over half of the electrical things in school make sounds." Is he right?

✂ -

Number of electrical things	What they do
Block graph to show what electricity is used for	

RESOURCE
SHEET

GROUPING SHEET PHOTOCOPIABLE

Name

Date

MATHS SKILLS FOR SCIENCE: YEARS 1&2

Name _____   Date _____

Name _____   Date _____

Title _____

Name   Date

	Total
	Total
	Total
	Total
	Total
	Total
	Total
	Total

Name _____

Date _____

Today I have completed an activity called

_____

This activity is about _____

_____

From this work I have learned _____

_____

Date _____

Today I have completed an activity called

_____

This activity is about _____

_____

From this work I have learned _____

_____

Date _____

Today I have completed an activity called

_____

This activity is about _____

_____

From this work I have learned _____

_____